SEARCHING
FOR THE
PROMISED LAND

SEARCHING
FOR THE
PROMISED LAND

AN AFRICAN AMERICAN'S
OPTIMISTIC ODYSSEY

CONGRESSMAN GARY FRANKS
The First Black Conservative Member of Congress

ReganBooks
An Imprint of HarperCollins*Publishers*

HarperCollins books may be purchased for educational, business, or sales promotional use. For information please write: Special Markets Department, HarperCollins Publishers, Inc., 10 East 53rd Street, New York, NY 10022.

FIRST EDITION

Designed by Laura Lindgren

Library of Congress Cataloging-in-Publication Data

Franks, Gary, 1953–
    Searching for the promised land : an African American's optimistic odyssey / by Gary Franks.
        p.   cm.
    ISBN 0-06-039156-1
    1. Franks, Gary, 1953–   . 2. Legislators—United States—Biography.   3. United States. Congress. House—Biography.   4. United States—Social policy—1993— 5. Afro-Americans—Politics and government.   6. United States—Race relations. I. Title.
    E840.8.F73   1996
    328.73'092—dc20   96-10714
    [B]

96 97 98 99 00 ❖/HC 10 9 8 7 6 5 4 3 2 1

In my parents, Richard and Jenary Franks,
God truly gave me the best.
I dedicate this book to them.

CONTENTS

PART FOUR Reforming Welfare

PART FIVE My Credo

FOREWORD

RACE AND ethnic origin is an issue that both divides and unites us as Americans. We come from so many different backgrounds, trace our roots to so many different parts of the world, practice so many different faiths and religions.

Yet we remain one people. We root for the same sports teams, go to similar high schools, compete for the same jobs, watch the same TV shows, use the same slang words, vote in the same elections, eat in the same fast-food restaurants, wear the same styles of clothing, pursue the same dreams.

Gary Franks is a man who embodies the best of those dreams. The son of a factory hand and a dietary specialist, Gary rose from humble beginnings through the aid and encouragement of a loving family to become one of the outstanding members of the U.S. House of Representatives.

His story defies all stereotypes. A young man who once had a cross burned on his front lawn, he has also been a bright and popular leader since high school. A scholarship student at Yale, he had his basketball career nearly ruined by a coach who wouldn't play black athletes. A young Republican with a broad vision, he climbed the ladder through an old-line, scandal-plagued political organization in Waterbury, Connecticut. A bright new leader with a serious concern for racial problems, he still managed to get elected in a blue-collar district that is 90 percent white.

Most remarkable has been Gary's experience in Congress. After arriving in 1990 as an eager freshman with new ideas for approaching racial problems, he was shunned by the liberal Democrats in the Congressional Black Caucus. Yet he held on— and has kept winning.

Gary's political career in Congress has been a profile in courage. His religious faith is inspiring. His devotion to his family is admirable. With most of his career still ahead of him, he has already become an outstanding role model for young Americans.

Dan Quayle
Forty-fourth Vice President of the United States

Searching for
the Promised Land

W HEN I WAS ten years old, I sat down in front of the television
set and watched Dr. Martin Luther King Jr. give a speech
before two hundred thousand people on the Capitol Mall. For a
few hours the world seemed to stand still.

"I have a dream," the historic pastor told the huge throng
gathered in front of him:

> I have a dream that the day will come when we judge a
> man not by the color of his skin but by the content of his
> character. I have a dream that this nation will rise up and
> live out the true meaning of its creed, "We hold these
> truths to be self-evident: that all men are created equal."
>
> And when we let freedom ring, when we let it ring
> from every village and every hamlet, from every state and
> every city, we will be able to speed up that day when all
> of God's children, black men and white men, Jews and
> Gentiles, Protestants and Catholics, will be able to join
> hands and sing in the words of the old Negro spiritual,
> "Free at last! Free at last! Thank God Almighty, we are free
> at last!"

No person of color has ever been able to forget that moment.

More than thirty years later, we find ourselves wondering just how much of Dr. King's vision remains. When the Reverend first spoke, the Civil Rights movement was in full flower. There was hope—passionate hope—that the institutional barriers and Jim Crow laws that had long relegated African Americans to second-class citizenship in America were at last coming down. That revolution, to a great degree, has been realized. There is still racism in America—I of all people can attest to this. But the outright segregation and vast stereotyping that was common thirty years ago has largely broken down. American blacks now succeed in all walks of life. There are black doctors, lawyers, bankers, stockbrokers, mayors, governors, and even presidential candidates. I myself am a member of the U.S. House of Representatives representing a district in which 90 percent of voters are white Americans.

Yet despite this progress, there is a sense of unease bordering on despair among American blacks that we have lost our way. When I talk with my fellow African Americans, I am inevitably told that something has gone tragically wrong. We had a vision and have somehow lost sight of it. We wanted material things and—although some of us remain among the poorest of Americans—we have certainly improved our lot. Yet somewhere along the line we lost the spiritual values that sustained us through so many long decades of slavery, poverty, Jim Crow, and beyond. Somewhere we lost the faith that told us we were a special people and that in compensation for our long suffering, our virtue would eventually be rewarded. Where did this passionate sense of moral direction go?

I believe our vision needs renewal. For far too long, too many black Americans have lived with the faith that the government is the chariot that is going to descend from the sky to rescue us. Somehow, somewhere, there is some federal program or bureaucracy that is going to lift us all into the promised land. Certainly, the government has played a major role in our success. Government has helped level the playing field so that African Americans can compete along with everyone else—that has been essential. But there are things that we can only do for ourselves. I think it's time we black Americans stopped looking to the government as the source of our redemption and started looking within our own souls.

*   *   *

In the following chapters I will be outlining my sense of what happened to our vision. I will begin with my life story—not only because it is the starting point of my personal vision, but because I think my odyssey through the American political system tells a lot about how we have become a far less race-conscious society. I am proud to be an African American and I count the concerns of black people as one of my foremost political responsibilities. But I am also proud to be American and I think it important to recognize that the opportunities I have encountered are available in few other countries of the world.

In part 2, I will deal with two of the most sensitive issues of our day: the role of Black Muslim extremism and the issue of affirmative action. These represent the polarization points in race relations from which I think we must find some way of pulling back.

In parts 3 and 4, I will outline my vision of the future. Black Americans need a blueprint for hope. In particular, this will mean confronting one of the most difficult issues of our time—the reform of the welfare system.

In the final section, I will talk about four principles that have sustained me through my long journey. It is here I want to bear witness to the role that religious faith has played in my life.

In April 1968, Dr. Martin Luther King Jr. gave another speech that many of us remember just as well as his Washington address. "I don't know what will happen now," he told an audience in Memphis:

> We've got some difficult days ahead. But it really doesn't matter to me now, because I've been to the mountaintop.
>
> Like anybody, I would like to live a long life. Longevity has its place, but I'm not concerned about that now. I just want to do God's will and He's allowed me to go up to the mountain. And I've looked over. And I've seen the Promised Land. . . .
>
> So I'm happy tonight. I'm not worried about anything. I'm not fearing any man. "Mine eyes have seen the glory of the coming of the Lord."

The next day he walked out onto a motel balcony in Memphis and was shot to death.

This book is written for all of us, black and white, Jew and Gentile, Protestant and Catholic, who are still searching for the promised land.

ACKNOWLEDGMENTS

As WITH everything else in my life, I have to start by thanking and acknowledging God for His direction, His inspiration, and His strength. Without God's help in this project and in my life, I would not be presenting this book for you to read.

I have been blessed in life with a copilot who has participated in nearly every step that I have taken since we met back in the 1980s, my wife, Donna. Her influence on this book as well as on my life has been profound. My children were also an inspiration. Often Azia, Jessica, or Gary Jr. would walk or crawl into the den to see me working. In so many ways, *Searching for the Promised Land* is written for them and for all our country's children.

The residents of Waterbury, Connecticut, must be acknowledged, along with the people of the Fifth Congressional District of Connecticut. I am very proud to be from Waterbury and honored to represent a district whose citizens have shown over and over again their willingness to be fair and color-blind in choosing their congressional representation.

Though they will be mentioned throughout the book, I also want to give special recognition to my mother, Jenary; and my brothers and sisters, Joan, Bonita, Richard, Ruth, and Marvin, for their help. My father, Richard, though he died in 1982, is a part of every line in this book.

My chief of staff, part-time campaign manager, godfather to my son, and best friend, Rick Genua, also deserves special recognition. Having shared in so many of the experiences recounted here, it was Rick who encouraged me over and over to pull it all together into a story.

This project has taken many twists and turns. It began with my encounter with Dr. Jeffrey Schwartz, my first editor and now my good friend. With nothing more than a verbal outline, he turned in an acceptable book proposal. Being both political and spiritual, this book reflects both of Jeffrey's passions. As a practicing psychiatrist, author of his own book, and avid Republican conservative, his input was enormous. That there is a book entitled *Searching for the Promised Land* is largely due to his influence.

I also want to thank my publisher, Judith Regan. She more than demonstrated why she has been so successful. Judith pushed and pulled more out of me than I thought I had to give. I truly enjoyed working with her.

I want to thank the ReganBooks and HarperCollins teams for walking me through the process and for their significant contribution toward its completion.

The first draft of this book was rejected by ReganBooks. It was not until I got Bill Tucker to join me on this project that it truly came to life. I thank Bill for the countless number of hours he spent helping me pull this manuscript together.

A special thanks is also due to my agent, B. K. Nelson; my transcriber, Lorraine Cipriano; my second father, Reverend John Blanchfield; and Jay Swayze.

It takes a lot to write a book, and I have been blessed.

INTRODUCTION

As a member of the United States Congress from the fifth district in Connecticut, I often visit local schools, talking to the children about their future. The results are usually discouraging but predictable.

Typically, I ask the children what they want to do when they grow up. Almost every black child mentions basketball, football, or baseball. They all want to be sports stars. The white youngsters will say they want to be bankers, accountants, chemists.

When I ask each group why they have chosen that profession, the white kids will say that they have uncles or neighbors who are accountants or chemists. The black youngsters will say they want to be sports professionals because they want to make a lot of money.

You get the feeling just from looking in the black kids' eyes that they don't have any knowledge of or role model for the kind of professions the white kids are talking about.

"Okay, what else might you be?" I ask the black kids.

There is a long pause and no answer.

"How about going to college?"

"Oh, yeah," someone will chuckle. "I guess I have to do that for awhile. Then after that I can be on the gravy train to make big bucks."

When I ask the white students the same question, they reply: "I have to go to college and maybe get a graduate degree or MBA or something like that."

I ask the students what they have as a backup in case their plans don't work out. The white students will quickly name another profession—biology, electrical engineering, the law. The black students will look at each other, perplexed, and then name another sport.

When I warn the black students that very few athletes ever make it to the professional level, they acknowledge that but say they know they can beat the odds. "I just have to keep practicing," they say. I remind them that no one in the history of Waterbury, Connecticut, my hometown and the largest town in my district, has ever played in the National Basketball Association. That does not faze them. I admire their confidence, but it saddens me that their dreams are so limited and their prospects for success so dim.

I do not remember my own dreams being so limited. When I was first elected to Congress in 1990, a former Yale classmate of mine told me he was disappointed to hear of my victory. He had made a wager several years ago and had now lost his bet.

"I had money on the Chicago Cubs," he told me.

"What does baseball have to do with my election to Congress?" I asked.

"Well, the odds were the Chicago Cubs would win the World Series before the Republican Party would elect a black to the U.S. House of Representatives."

In 1990 I became the first black Republican in the House in nearly sixty years. I was also the first black conservative ever to serve in Congress. At the time I was thirty-seven years old. I was elected from a Connecticut congressional district that is 90 percent white.

I hold the dubious distinction of being the only African American who has been threatened and attacked by both the Ku Klux Klan and the NAACP. Even the Congressional Black Caucus attempted to throw me out—as I will relate later—because my views on the issues were different from theirs.

What has motivated me and kept me going? I have lived most of my life according to four principles. I often try to convey these to young people, particularly African American youth, who face a special burden in our society. But they apply to anyone who is trying to improve their lot in life. Here they are.

First, you must put God first in your life. As long as I can remember, I have attended church regularly. When I was in grade school, I sat in the first seat, on the far right, just behind the deacons, in Grace Baptist Church every single Sunday. While in high school, I stopped by the chapel before starting school every day.

In the Catholic high school I attended, we began every single class with a prayer. I didn't object, even though I was not Catholic. Throughout my grade school years I remember experiencing a moment of silence or reciting the Lord's Prayer every morning as the school day began.

Since then, I have started each day with a visit to church, a half-hour of Bible study, or both. This has given me the confidence, the inner strength and guidance I needed to defeat what otherwise might have seemed like insurmountable odds.

In early 1994, Rick Genua, an old high school friend who now serves as my chief of staff, discovered that I always go to church at some time during the day. Rick, a deacon in the Catholic Church, now often accompanies me. At first, he was surprised that I did this on a regular basis, but now it is a habit we share.

Many people have said of me, "Gary Franks has a way of pulling rabbits out of hats." Or they say, "Gary Franks is just so lucky!" I've replied many times, "If an atheist followed me around for one year, I would make him a believer." That's why, when I hear people discuss a moment of silent prayer in school, I cannot see how any American could oppose putting God first in one's life.

Second, you must believe in yourself. You must be willing to dream. You must set goals—both for the short and long run. This principle is one that so many of today's young African Americans fail to appreciate.

Unfortunately, many people believe those who tell them that they won't amount to anything. I remember people telling me that I would never make it into Catholic school, I could never attend an Ivy League college. My older brothers and sisters—I have five of them—heard grown-ups give them many reasons why they couldn't do a wide range of things. Yet they all excelled anyway.

Today, when I'm addressing young grade school and high school students, I tell them they must believe in themselves, no matter how much others try to discourage them. To illustrate my point, I walk them through a little history lesson. I tell them that many people doubted Abraham Lincoln could ever become president of the United States. After all, he had only served in Congress for one term and failed as a candidate for the U.S. Senate. How could he think of running for the presidency? Yet he ignored the detractors and ended up in the White House.

The press and political professionals told Franklin Delano Roosevelt that he was a good governor of New York but that there was no way that a person with a physical disability could have the stamina or image to run for president of the United States. FDR ignored the naysayers and went on to serve longer than any president in U.S. history.

According to the conventional wisdom, John F. Kennedy could not have become president. He was too young and, as a Catholic, too closely tied to the Pope. JFK disregarded such sentiments and beat Richard Nixon on his trek to 1600 Pennsylvania Avenue. To this day, Kennedy's spirit remains with us, especially through institutions such as the space program and the Peace Corps.

The experts dismissed Ronald Reagan's chances, too. "Well, Ron," he surely heard, "you're getting up there in age. You did a fine job as governor of California, but you're too old. Why not think about retirement?" So what did Ronald Reagan do? He ignored this advice and won consecutive electoral landslides. He left office as the oldest individual ever to serve as president. He also was the first president to complete two terms since Dwight David Eisenhower.

Now let's bring the lesson closer to home, I tell my audiences. When I ran for Congress, people remarked, "You're a nice guy, but you're going to lose."

"Why?" I wondered.

"It's very obvious, Gary. You're black."

"Yes," I answered. "I've known that for a number of years."

"Well, you don't understand. White people aren't going to vote for you, because you're black," the wise men told me. "Worse yet, black people aren't going to vote for you, because you're a Republican. You just don't have a chance."

I just overlooked such nonsense, ran hard, and—as I will relate in the following chapters—eventually prevailed. People will always try to convince you that you cannot do something that seems difficult or improbable. You must not let them discourage you. You must dream big dreams.

Third, you must always work hard. There are so many people these days who will not do a certain type of work. They act as if they have a right to an easy job. They refuse to take certain entry-level positions. They look for the fast buck and take the path of least resistance.

After I was elected to Congress, a reporter from *Reader's Digest* asked me, "Who was your first boss?"

I had to think for a minute before I finally answered. "Everyone was, I guess."

My first job was at Waterbury Hospital, where my mother had worked for many years. I washed pots, pans, and toilets, mopped floors, and cleaned up the kitchen. On a good day, I got to wash the dishes. Once in a while, I got to take food to the patients. Yet at sixteen, I was very happy. I did everything to the best of my ability and was proud of the praise I got from others when I did my job well.

Did I enjoy the work? Yes. Did I look forward to having the same job for the next thirty years? No. But I knew I was proving myself. I was earning my own way. My employers were willing to pay me for what I did. By bringing home a paycheck, I was able to help my parents meet their expenses as well.

That was another big factor—my family. My father worked hard at factory jobs all his life, even though he had barely learned to read and write. My mother worked at Waterbury Hospital, as did all of my brothers and sisters at one point or another. When I started work there, I knew my performance reflected on my whole family. I was not going to let them down.

I also tell young audiences about my experience at Yale University. When I got there, I told myself, "Gee, I'm going to school with all these geniuses." I was a little intimidated. Then I saw how all these geniuses performed their wonders. After class, Monday through Thursday, you would be hard-pressed to find an empty seat in the library. These young geniuses did well because they worked hard. On weekends, of course, it was different. Everybody let their hair down. But during the week, people cracked the books.

Sometimes I tell young students about my experience as an all-state basketball player. "You were just gifted," they tell me. "You could jump so high. You could shoot so well. It was easy for you."

I tell them, "How about running a mile or two each day in a fifteen-pound weight jacket and ankle weights? Do you think that would improve your speed and jumping ability?" I know from my career at Yale how much my so-called shooting ability depended on nothing but practice—as I will relate later. Without keeping up, I could be plain awful.

Nothing worthwhile or long-lasting can be achieved without hard work. I always remember a quote from U.S. Senator Bill Bradley during his basketball days at Princeton. He said his father would tell him, "Son, when you're not out practicing, someone else is. And when you meet that person, he's going to beat you." That's the way I've lived my life.

The fourth principle is to be thankful to God for whatever you achieve. This is probably the most difficult one of all. You may think that dreaming big dreams and working hard for them will get you whatever you want. But it doesn't always happen. Sometimes you fall short or don't prevail. That's when you grow the most. Though you may not think it's fair that you didn't achieve everything you hoped, you have to let God lead you. The only way to do that is to show your gratitude to Him for whatever He allows you to achieve.

I tell students my biggest victory was a defeat. They look at me funny. Then I tell them about my race for Connecticut state comptroller in 1986.

I was holding my first elected office as a Waterbury city alderman at the time. Then I decided to try for state comptroller. I was the first black Republican in Connecticut ever nominated for a state constitutional position. My opponent, Ed Cardwell, was a popular three-term incumbent. Nobody said as much, but the expectation was that I was just there to lose. Nominating an African American would "balance the ticket." It would look good, even though nobody expected me to be a serious candidate.

At the start of the campaign, Republican State Chairman Tom D'Amore pulled me aside and said, "Now Gary, remember, your areas will be Bridgeport, New Haven, Stamford, and Hartford." These are the only towns with sizable black populations.

"But there are one hundred sixty-five other towns in the state," I protested.

"Don't worry," he reassured me. "We'll take care of them for you."

The implication was clear: Bring us in a few black votes, and let it go at that. We especially don't want you running around white neighborhoods where a minority candidate will turn people off.

I did just the opposite. I campaigned in the toniest neighborhoods of the state. I didn't forget Hartford and Bridgeport, but I tramped through Greenwich, Old Lyme, Glastonbury, Wilton, and West Hartford. When the votes were counted, I only lost by six percentage points. The gubernatorial candidate lost by sixteen, and the rest of the ticket did even worse. As a one-year alderman and the youngest person in the history of Connecticut ever to run for statewide office, I had led the ticket.

During the early returns, I actually thought for awhile that I might win. Only when the big-city vote came in did I eventually fall behind. At first I was disappointed. Then I fell to my knees and thanked God for allowing me to compete. Although I didn't realize it at the time, my defeat was actually a great victory. It showed that I could appeal to a wide variety of voters and opened the path for me to run for the Fifth Congressional District four years later. Only by thanking God did I show my appreciation and respect for what I had actually accomplished.

The same thing happened during my basketball career at college. After being an all-star high school player and an outstanding freshman at Yale, I spent most of the rest of my career riding the bench. The reason—as I will relate later—had to do with my coach. I was angry and spent a lot of time sitting around the dining table bitching and moaning about my playing time.

Then one day, Gary Rinck, a six-foot-seven-inch, 220-pound player from Chicago, came hobbling into the dining hall on crutches. He had hurt himself in practice and was out for the entire season. After listening to me whine a bit more, he finally said, "Gary, all you've done all year is complain."

"Well, it's not fair," I shot back. "I should be playing more."

"Gary, I practiced hard all summer and now my whole season is shot. That's not fair, either."

I realized he was right. I had much more to be thankful for

than I realized. From that incident at Yale in 1972 through the moment when I dropped to my knees on election night of 1986, I have made it a practice to thank God for my opportunities, no matter how meager they might seem. Looking back, I see those two moments as pivotal in shaping my attitude toward life. It has helped me weather bad times as well as prepare for the good ones. I have expressed my appreciation to God for whatever He has brought me. In every instance, He has helped me do better.

Putting God first, dreaming big dreams, working hard, and thanking God for what He has brought you—these are the four principles that have served me through life.

"But isn't it difficult to show thanks when you've been defeated?" some kid always asks.

"It may be at first," I tell him. "But you get better with practice."

WHY THE GOP?

I am frequently asked why I am a member of the Republican Party. Some would joke that a black Republican is an oxymoron. Well, I have been a Republican since the late 1970s. Maybe it was those high interest rates, high unemployment, and high inflation brought on by the Carter years that pushed me over the brink. But all the blame or credit should not go to former President Jimmy Carter. The failures of the Great Society of Lyndon Johnson truly deserve acknowledgment as well. The tax-and-spend, big-government approach of the Democratic Party is simply not appealing to me.

I have a little speech that I often give to black audiences who are skeptical about my party affiliation.

"How many of you would favor less taxes so that you could keep more money in your own pocket instead of giving it to Uncle Sam?" I ask. Every hand in the room goes up.

"How many of you believe that if a person takes the life of another individual he should be subject to losing his own life as well?" Every hand goes up.

"How many of you believe the government should spend no more money each year than it takes in so we aren't passing on the bills to our grandchildren?" Every hand goes up.

"How many believe every youngster should have the right to choose which school he or she would like to attend whether or not it lies in his or her school district?" Every hand goes up.

"How many are in favor of reforming the welfare system?" Just about every hand goes up.

"How many have a problem with beginning each day in school with a moment of silent reflection?" No hands go up.

"Well, congratulations," I tell them, "you are all honorary Republicans."

They generally look around at each other in amazement and say, "Well, I never . . . "

Republicans and African Americans go back a long way. They don't call it "the party of Lincoln" for nothing. During and after Reconstruction, every African American elected to office at both the state and national level was a Republican. Of those blacks who served in Congress, all were with the GOP.

The Jim Crow rebellion in the South put an end to this representation, but Republicans remained loyal to African Americans, even though there was little electoral payoff. Theodore Roosevelt entertained Booker T. Washington at the White House and appointed several blacks to government positions. (Woodrow Wilson, a Virginia Democrat, promptly kicked them all out again.) Oscar Stanton DePriest, a Republican from Chicago, became the first black elected to the House of Representatives in the twentieth century in 1928.

However, with the growth of big government, blacks began slowly shifting their allegiance to the Democratic Party. DePriest lost his seat to Democrat Arthur Mitchell in 1934. From that moment until my election in 1990, the only African Americans to serve in Congress were Democrats.

In the 1960 Kennedy-Nixon presidential election, Richard Nixon received 40 percent of the black vote. If that were still happening today, the Republicans would have a lock on the White House. In fact, getting only 20 percent of the black vote would elect a Republican president every time. When Republicans pass this threshold in gubernatorial and big-city mayoral elections, they win almost every time.

It is truly a shame that a president still loses 90 percent of the black vote after doing all of the following: passing a civil rights bill with the largest margin in history, hiring more blacks in his administration than any other president, nominating and strongly supporting a black Justice to the Supreme Court, placing a black in Dwight D. Eisenhower's position as chairman of the Joint Chiefs of Staff, and fighting hard to promote a two-party system for African Americans by encouraging and supporting black Republicans. Yet that is what happened to George Bush.

In twelve years as governor of Arkansas, Bill Clinton failed to pass either a civil rights bill or an anti–housing discrimination bill, leaving Arkansas as one of only two states (Mississippi is the other) without such basic laws.

No political party is all good or bad. African Americans must seek the truth and be willing to evaluate objectively the candidates and issues of both parties.

PART ONE

MY STORY

Childhood Memories

HAD IT NOT BEEN for a family dispute, I might have grown up in the South rather than New England.

My grandfather, Charles Franks, was a tobacco farmer in Maysville, North Carolina, and deacon at the White Oak Baptist Church. Thanks to his hard work, plus that of his twelve children, the farm increased in size and abundance. Even today, tobacco still grows on our old homestead.

My father, Richard Franks, was one of Charles's youngest and strongest sons. He and my mother, Jenary, met at the Union Baptist Church, in nearby Jacksonville, which my maternal grandmother, Minnie Petteway, helped found. After my parents married, Grandpa Charles asked them to stay in North Carolina to help run the farm.

As with most rural people, Grandma Caroline and Grandpa Charles believed their girls ought to be educated while boys worked in the fields. "Being educated," of course, merely meant learning to read and write. None of my aunts and uncles ever went to college and only one graduated from high school. My father didn't do either. Because of his strength as a "human tractor," he never had the chance to go to high school. He had a sixth-grade education and barely learned to read or write.

Several of my aunts and uncles also worked the farm, and after a few years, the conflicts and tensions finally got to everybody. One day several years before I was born—so the story goes—my oldest sister, Joan, got into a fight with one of her cousins. The cousin's mother, my Aunt Hattie, started dressing her down severely. My mother walked up the stairs and right into the middle of it. That set off a huge battle between my mother and my aunt.

That was the end for my mom. Living on a farm with two other families and all sorts of extended family members passing through all the time was too much for her patience. She insisted we move. In 1936, at her suggestion, my father decided to move to Waterbury, Connecticut, where my mom had an uncle and an older brother. Good-paying manufacturing jobs were plentiful at the time. For more than a decade, my family lived in a three-family house on Orange Street in the North End of Waterbury that had been purchased by my mother's brother, Peter Petteway. Then in 1951, they purchased our family pride and joy and what was to become the beginning of our climb up the economic ladder—a three-family home. On February 9, 1953, I was born.

I was the sixth and youngest child of what was a very close family. My father was forty-one years old when I was born and my mother was forty. As a latecomer, I was a bit of a surprise. At first, my mother was thought to have a tumor. Then she was finally diagnosed as being pregnant. That was me.

My parents had just bought the house in a well-kept neighborhood in the North End, occupied by homeowners. Today the area has changed considerably. Our street was called Camp Terrace. It wasn't really a street so much as a long driveway off Orange Street, one of the main roads through the neighborhood. It wasn't wide enough to be an official street and even today it is not listed on most city maps. Yet to us it was a wonderful place. There were four houses, all three-deckers. The road led up a hill. From the top you had a beautiful view of all of Waterbury. On the Fourth of July, when the city government set off fireworks, you could see all of Waterbury lit up by the "rockets' red glare."

For many people, Richard and Jenary Franks were pushovers. Anyone who visited our house could always expect a warm meal and a place to lay their head. More often than not, that would be my parents' bed. I can remember relative after relative arriving at our door. Many lived with us for years until they were married or able to get something of their own.

At times, my siblings would grumble about my parents' generosity. But it never deterred them from doing what they thought was right. "A closed hand also allows nothing in," my mother would say. "The more you give the more you will receive. You can never be used. You are only building up blessings with God."

To this day, I am still not sure in which room I slept the first few years of my life. With three older sisters and two older brothers, along with the regular live-in relatives, the five-room apartment on the second floor was always crowded. At the time, it didn't bother me at all. Our home just seemed like an exciting place where something was always going on.

My three sisters shared one bedroom. My two older brothers shared a family room that was converted to a bedroom every night. My earliest memories are of sleeping on a sofabed in my parents' bedroom. The front room was the dressiest part of the house, yet at night even this was converted to a bedroom if there was a relative sleeping over. While I was still young, my cousin Ulysses Grant (Buddy) Pollock arrived from North Carolina. His mother and father had both died. He occupied the front room and quickly became my third brother in our family.

What made it possible for us to pay for the house, of course, were the two rental apartments above and below us. The downstairs apartment was rented for many years to my mother's relatives, the Gatlings. The upstairs was rented to the Washingtons, who became good friends. With all these people around, I had all the day care I needed. I can still remember coming home from school every day and staying at my cousins' apartment downstairs while waiting for my parents to come home from work.

In those days, there were plenty of jobs for manual laborers in Waterbury's brass and copper mills. At six feet, 210 pounds, my father had no trouble making a good living. Having graduated from high school, my mother was also able to get a better job than many other people who migrated up from the South. She worked for ten years at Uniroyal, known as "the Rubber Shop," and Scovill before spending another twenty-five years working at Waterbury Hospital as a dietary specialist.

Because my brothers and sisters were so much older than me, I spent a lot of time as a youngster playing by myself. I had an imaginary baseball league filled with baseball cards. I handicapped the players by using statistics to determine whether they were home-run hitters or singles hitters. Today my brothers and sisters tell me that these games with imaginary friends and imaginary players were one of the dominant aspects of my young life.

I needed it. One thing we were never allowed to do as children was watch much television. Every time my father caught us watching, he would turn it off. "They've already got theirs," he would say, wagging his finger at the blank screen. "It's still yours to get."

From the earliest days, I knew the most important thing in our household was studying. As a man with no schooling, my father believed the most important thing in life was education.

Both my older sisters were already schoolteachers. This helped me immensely. I can remember going out into the hallway to watch my sister Bonita study. She would hide herself there to get away from the noise. She eventually finished in the top five of her high school class. Bonita went on to get her Ph.D. from Penn State. She taught at the University of Tennessee, Temple, and is now at Bloomsburg University in Pennsylvania.

In fact, all my older siblings found success through education. My oldest sister, Joan, graduated from Howard University, received her master's from the University of Bridgeport, and a Ph.D. from Wayne State. Today she teaches guidance counseling at the University of Virginia.

My oldest brother, Richard, graduated from North Carolina Central College, received a master's from Howard, and reached the rank of colonel in the Army Reserves. Today he is a psychiatric social worker for the state of Connecticut.

My youngest sister, Ruth, graduated from North Carolina Central, received a master's from Central Connecticut State University in New Britain, then returned to NCC for a law degree. She taught for many years in the Waterbury public schools and is now vice president of the State Street Bank.

My youngest brother, Marvin, graduated from Voorhees College in South Carolina and received a master's from Southern Connecticut State University. He has taught sixth grade in Ansonia, Connecticut, and coaches the girls' high school softball team.

My father even managed to send our cousin Buddy Pollock to college. Although he never completed his studies, Buddy still remembers vividly going to North Carolina A&T with Jesse Jackson. Today he is a successful carpenter.

None of this came easily. My oldest brother, Richard, was so shy as a child that when called on to make an address or recite lines in Sunday school, he wouldn't respond. "Now we will hear a recital from Richard Franks," the Sunday school principal would announce. Richard wouldn't budge. "Now we will hear a recital from Richard Franks!" he would say a little louder. Richard would stay thumbtacked to his chair. "All right," he would relent, glaring at my brother, "we will now hear a recital from Robert Jones." Yet Richard eventually came out of his shell to become a colonel in the U.S. Army. Several of my brothers and sisters got off to slow starts and people in the neighborhood said they would never amount to much. Yet they all persevered.

So how did the children of a nearly illiterate, farm-bred factory worker become so successful? My parents always insisted that we could do well if we just kept trying. The discipline I learned as a youngster always helped me concentrate on my schoolwork. Having seen all my brothers and sisters progress, I knew education was the most important thing in the world. Today I am the only sibling in my family with only *one* college degree. Only after I was elected to Congress did my mother finally stop asking me when I was going to go back to school!

Another big part of my education was helping my father in the real estate business. As he grew more familiar with banks and mortgages, my father realized he could move us to a new house while keeping the old house as a rental. We still own the old three-decker. (It would eventually play a big part in my first congressional campaign.)

Because of my father's limited formal education, I became his real estate "accountant." I still remember tagging along, writing out rent receipts or penning gentle reminders to tenants who had forgotten to pay. It gave me a sense of business that is still with me today.

One of the greatest joys we had as adults was presenting my father with a new car. He had owned many used cars but never had a new one. On Christmas Day in 1976, we parked the car on the front lawn, right outside the living room window. Then, with a dramatic flourish, we pulled back the curtains and presented him with the keys. This was the first time we had ever seen our father cry . . . with tears of joy. To this day, my mother still keeps the car in our garage.

I also remember fighting to help my father when the Chase Brass and Copper Company was closing down, leaving him with a severe medical condition that we claimed resulted from his employment, although this was disputed by the company. Although I had just graduated from Yale, I jumped in with both feet, negotiating with not only the Waterbury office but the parent company in Cleveland. Ultimately, I secured a settlement of ten thousand dollars for him from Chase Brass and Copper Company. It was more than my father had ever made from his annual salary. He used the check to pay off his mortgage—a very proud moment for him. At the time, he mentioned that the bank— First Federal (now known as Webster Bank)—had been willing to lend him the money to buy a house in a white neighborhood when few other banks were willing to lend to African Americans at all. To this day, it leaves a fond memory in my heart.

Only a few years later, I was literally carrying my father to his car, picking him up out of bed and taking him to the hospital, where he would undergo kidney dialysis three times a week. Many times I had to fight the tears. I kept thinking about how not many years before my father had been carrying me. Once a strong man of over 200 pounds, he weighed less than 135 at the end.

My father died in 1982 at age seventy, five years after his original diagnosis. I was twenty-nine years old. My mother, God bless her, is still with us. One of the biggest regrets of my life is that my father did not live to see me in my political career. Yet I can imagine his reaction. He would nod his head, mildly congratulatory but mildly disapproving as well. "You're doing good, Gary," he would say. "But don't let up now. You've still got a lot of important work ahead of you."

It's Hard to Forget Where You Came from When You've Never Really Left

I WILL NEVER FORGET one summer evening in 1963 I spent with my three cousins from Durham, North Carolina, when I was ten years old. The whole family set off to see a movie. In those days, the Lakewood Drive-In offered a recreation area for children. Right up front, just beneath the giant white screen, kids played on swings, slides, and sandbox. It was fun and got us out of our parents' hair as well.

With twilight creeping upon us, I said to my three little cousins, "Let's run up and jump on the swings." Burnes (a boy my age we called Junior) and his two little sisters, Marla Anne, nine, and Sharon, six, all hopped out of the car and dashed toward the play area. Just steps away from the monkey bars, so close we could feel drawn in by the other kids' laughter and screams of joy, Sharon suddenly slowed down and burst into tears. "We can't go in there," she screamed.

"What's wrong?" I asked, wondering if she might have eyed a

wasp's nest or something. Her brother ran back to reassure her.

"We can't! You know we can't, Junior," she continued to scream.

"What's wrong?" I demanded. She was starting to scare me.

"All those kids are white," she explained tearfully. "We can't play where white kids are."

I was stunned. I had seen many racist incidents on television and knew about the work of freedom fighters such as Dr. Martin Luther King Jr. and Roy Wilkins. But somehow I had never made the connection with something as familiar as my own playground. Granted, we would be the only black children in the group, yet that had never been a problem. I was taken aback by the utter terror in Sharon's voice.

Finally we convinced her to join us. As she played on the equipment, she kept looking timidly at the white children, as if at any moment they might tell her to leave. But as time went on, she seemed to realize that the other children saw her as just another child on the swing set. She loosened up a bit and enjoyed herself.

It gratified me that evening as I kept a close eye on Sharon to see that those kids did not see one another as black or white individuals. Perhaps their parents had told them lies about black people, but that was not apparent in their eyes or in the eyes of the parents who stood nearby. Even today, when I see black, white, and brown kids playing together, my mind flashes back to that night when my petrified cousin stood frozen in front of the playground because white kids were smiling and playing there.

The North End, where we lived until I was nine years old, was a predominantly black section of Waterbury. I spent my first four years in school at Walsh Elementary. I forget the exact ethnic makeup, but there were a number of white children in my classrooms. Today, Walsh is so heavily black that the city has opted to bus white students into the neighborhood. It has become a magnet school, offering a strict discipline that attracts high-achieving students of all colors.

In 1962, we bought a house in Town Plot, the area where the founders of the city originally settled and which was predominantly white. Some of our friends in the North End warned us we would be living in a very different environment. "You may never want to come back and see us," they said.

I thought little of these comments at the time, but I've heard it over and over again as I rose through city and state politics. I've come to know what they mean. *People want to be sure you haven't forgotten where you came from.* My reply is always the same: "It's hard to forget where you came from when you've never really left."

I still attend Baptist church services in my old neighborhood, even though my wife is Catholic. I've always been proud that the core of my electoral support has been in the black community. Several of my closest friends today are people I knew from Camp Terrace. Reggie Beamon, the godfather of my daughter Jessica, is himself a Democratic state representative. His brother Mickey was in my wedding. And Richard Knight, one of my oldest friends, was the executive assistant in my congressional office. That's pretty good for a bunch of kids who used to amuse themselves by lining up empty soda bottles on a wall and trying to break them by throwing rocks.

The school in Town Plot was called B. W. Tinker Elementary. Before moving we toured the neighborhood by car several times. I saw few black kids. "What's it going to be like being the only black kid in class?" I asked my mother. "It won't be any different," she shrugged. "School is school."

Sure enough, when I started school the following September, I was the only black child in my grade. In fact, there was only one other black family, the Rhineharts, in the entire elementary school.

Miss Hubbard, my fourth-grade teacher, was a stocky, bespectacled lady in her late fifties with a face as loving as Santa's without the beard. She and many of her students were initially curious about my presence in the classroom. But I never hesitated to engage them in conversation and we quickly became very comfortable with each other.

Some might imagine I felt an undue pressure as the only black in the room. But I never experienced any anxiety. What I remember best about Miss Hubbard was her insistence that we always stand up and speak loudly when giving presentations to our classmates. The discipline she gave me in that class has helped me throughout my career as a politician. The ability to stand up and address your peers is something many adults find exceedingly difficult and intimidating. I just made my presentation like everyone else. To my classmates, there was never any problem.

My very warm, positive experience at B.W. Tinker from fourth through eighth grades truly helped shape me as a black American. Never in those years did I feel uncomfortable or intimidated by my white peers. Neither did my peers display any degree of racism toward me. Their parents may have had different feelings, but as far as the children of Waterbury were concerned, ours was a very friendly environment, one in which I was allowed to achieve and excel.

During my four years at Tinker, I was either the top student, the runner-up, or the best male student in my class. Whenever there were elections for any type of position, I was always elected. I served many times as team captain or class president

Because I lived so far from the school, I stayed there through lunch hour. In my first year there, three of my friends and I approached the assistant janitor with a proposition. We would do part of his work if he allowed us access to the gym during lunch. We also convinced the lunch monitor to go along. We did this the entire five years I was at B.W. Tinker. It would take us twenty minutes to empty the classroom wastebaskets and clean the hall floors. Then we would make our way to the gym to play basket-ball.

One day as we were emptying wastebaskets, my friend called me into an empty classroom. "Look, there are our test papers," he said excitedly. They were piled on the teacher's desk. They had not been graded.

"Let's fix them so we can get an A," he whispered.

I was tempted but the Christian side of me said no. "We can't do that," I told him. "We'd be stealing a grade."

He disagreed. He proceeded to fix his test so he had all the right answers. Then he further tempted me by telling me he had looked at my test paper and I would probably get a C.

"I'd rather get an honest C than a dishonest A," I told him.

Three days later, the teacher announced that she would have to give us the test all over again. She had misplaced our first papers. Since it would all be the same material, it shouldn't make a difference.

That left my friend with two problems: (1) he would probably do poorly on this test and (2) if the teacher found the original test, she would discover he had had a remarkable lapse of memory. I suspect she knew what had happened.

As for me, I had been so disappointed in my original performance that I went back and studied the material all the harder. I ended up with an A minus.

I knew right then that following God and being honest was the right thing to do.

The friendships I made at Tinker have grown and endured. Dorothy Genua, my seventh-grade teacher, and her son Rick became my good friends. They were the first white family to invite me into their home. Before long, I was coming and going as if I were one of their own. They took me to University of Connecticut basketball games. Today, Dorothy is my executive assistant and Rick is my congressional chief of staff. Thirty years ago, when I was in seventh grade, I was Rick's playground monitor. In 1993, he was at my side when I was confronted by an angry mob of demonstrators in Savannah, Georgia—an episode I will relate in chapter 11.

None of these people ever patronized me or even made me feel uncomfortable. They never focused on the only thing that made us different—the way we looked. The welcome I received at Tinker helped me recognize that God created us all equal in His sight and no group of people is privileged or better than any other. No matter our color, the makeups of our families are very similar. Moms want the same things for their kids, no matter in what part of town they live. There was a lesson those of us across Waterbury came to learn: *White people won't automatically do better than you because you're black and they're white. Work hard, get good grades, and you can succeed.*

Although things were going well for me at school, I couldn't say the same for us and our neighbors.

On the day after Halloween, 1964, I woke up in our home on Town Plot and wandered downstairs. We had been living there for two years. My father sat at the kitchen counter in his plaid work shirt eating blueberry pancakes, a treat we enjoyed once a week. My mother paced back and forth between the stove and the refrigerator in her all-white Waterbury Hospital uniform, which she often wore around the house, even on weekends. They spoke in hushed tones and seemed to be bothered by something they had heard outside the night before.

"Last night was just Halloween," Mom said. "It's like all Halloweens."

My father shook his head. "Halloween never used to be like this. These people are crazy."

Still puzzled at what was bothering them, I stepped into the backyard to throw out the trash. I found myself face-to-face with a giant cross. It was very tall and leaning between our house and the garage. It was charred and smelled of smoke. I walked back into the house and told Mom and Dad I'd found a discarded cross in our backyard that looked just like the ones I'd seen on television.

"It's all right, son," they reassured me. "It's just a prank." But I knew it wasn't.

I was stunned. I had heard of things like this happening in the South, but I couldn't believe it could happen in Connecticut. Later, my parents told me the whole story. Our dog, Tiny, was awakened by noises in the middle of the night. Half-collie and half–German shepherd, he was a good watchdog. He barked and ran feverishly up and down the staircase until he stirred my parents from their sleep. At first, no one knew what was going on. Then the phone rang. It was Mr. Lusso, our neighbor diagonally across the street. He was calling to tell us that a cross was ablaze in our front yard. It had been burning quite a while.

My father always suspected one of our neighbors either put the cross on our lawn or knew who did. The cross was planted precisely where we couldn't see it from inside the house. Only someone who lived very close to us would have known about that blind spot. We also realized later what might have kicked off these incidents after two peaceful years. Another black family, the Bakers, had just moved into the neighborhood.

The cross burning was followed by threat-filled phone calls

virtually every evening for the next two months. It got so bad that my mother and father refused to let me answer the phone. My mother or father would pick up the phone, greet the caller, then say: "We're not moving.... Over my dead body will I move.... I'll spill every drop of blood before leaving my home." Then they'd slam the handset back on the cradle, so that the small bell inside would ring and slowly fade away.

The smallest incidents became scary and frightening. I remember one night looking outside our window with my brothers and sisters, watching my father go to work at the Chase Brass and Copper factory. Two cars were coming up the road as my father pulled to the end of the driveway. The first car went past, but the second slowed to let my father pull out.

Watching from the window, we were all petrified. "Don't get in the middle! Don't get between them!" my sisters screamed as my father's car drove out of sight. We were terrified somebody was plotting something against him. Only when we called work a half hour later and found he had arrived safely did things calm down.

We lived in a secluded rural area surrounded by woods, and every night became a scheduled horror. It was not unusual to see white people hunting for pheasant and deer, walking through the woods with shotguns cradled in their arms. We had never worried before, but now the fear of a shotgun blast or a Molotov cocktail through our windows kept us awake half the night.

One day we heard a thunderous noise and ran outside to see what had happened. A medium-size mixed-breed dog had been gunned down on our front lawn. When the police arrived, they theorized that whoever shot the dog thought it was a deer. They pursued it no further. The dog just happened to belong to the Bakers, the other black family that had just moved into the neighborhood.

I started feeling grateful that my father kept a rifle in the garage along with two shotguns and plenty of ammunition in the house. When he heard suspicious sounds outside, he would go to the window with his shotgun, just in case. While we all had plenty to fear, my dad remained defiant—and well armed.

By mid-December, my brothers and sisters were all home

from school for the holidays. One morning I went to the mailbox, expecting to find a few Christmas cards. Instead, I found a small, bright-red bundle. It was a sheet drenched in fresh blood. As I slowly pulled it out, I discovered a dead possum swaddled inside. I dropped the deadly package in horror and ran back into the house.

I felt myself tremble as I told my folks what had happened. The whole family came out and saw the bloody carcass. There was a note attached to the sheet, just like a ransom letter in a mystery movie. Cutout letters from magazines and newspapers were pasted together into a terrifying message: "Niggers, you will be like this dead possum if you don't move." Later, we got an offensive telephone call telling us that the possum's fate would be ours if we didn't move out by the weekend.

Once again, we called the police. To our surprise, we learned that by placing the note in the mailbox, the perpetrators had committed a federal offense. This brought in the FBI. The whole investigation took on a different tone. Before the end of the weekend, they had apprehended the culprits. One was a young man in his early twenties whose home I passed every day on my way to school. Had I not been taking the bus, I would have been walking past his house. I did not recognize the name of the other defendant. Before the arrests, we sat all that weekend waiting for our house to blow up or be set afire. We felt like prisoners in our own home.

The FBI and local police decided to protect us and increased their surveillance. They obviously didn't want this thing to become an embarrassment for Waterbury. As the story popped up in the local papers, Italian and Jewish neighbors—some of them total strangers—came visiting to offer us support.

After that, things calmed down. Not until my first campaign for Congress did I again encounter any overt signs of racial hostility in my hometown.

THREE

~✿✿✿~

Sacred Heart

Oₙₒₑ I GRADUATED from Tinker, I attended Sacred Heart High School in Waterbury. My parents wanted me to go to Taft, an exclusive prep boarding school, but I had my heart set on Sacred Heart—partly because they had just won the state basketball championship. Somehow, though, I failed to take the school's entrance exam in time. My sister Joan made an appointment for me to see Father John Blanchfield, the principal, hoping he could navigate me around this omission. It turned out to be more than just an appointment. From almost the moment we met, Father Blanchfield became a second father to me. No other man has done more to help me in my career. He married my wife and me at the Immaculate Conception Church in 1990. Our friendship and true love for each other have been constant to this day.

I remember finding him on the top floor of the three-story schoolhouse. The halls were filled with teenagers in blue-and-white uniforms running in every direction with huge stacks of books under their arms. There, in their midst, stood Father Blanchfield, an imposing figure at six feet, hands on his hips and a cigar in his mouth. If a boy's sideburns were too long or a girl's dress skirt too short, his voice boomed out the standards by which all Sacred Heart students were expected to live.

Our meeting turned out to be a short one. As I walked up to him, he said, "You must be the Franks kid."

"Yes, Father." I nodded.

"I hear you want to come to Sacred Heart. Well, do you have something to show me?" I handed him my report card. He looked at my marks: straight A's from top to bottom. He looked back at me, glanced at my sister, and said, "You're in." He knew Tinker School and realized that good grades there meant something.

Sacred Heart was not free. Although we were not wealthy, my father and mother pinched and scratched so they could pay the annual tuition of a few hundred dollars plus buy the books I would be needing for classes. These sacrifices and the honors I earned on my report card eventually paid off. In my sophomore year, I was granted a full scholarship for the balance of my years at Sacred Heart. It was named the Dr. Martin Luther King Jr. Scholarship.

Of the one thousand students at Sacred Heart, only three or four of us were black. It never bothered me and didn't seem to bother anyone else either. I got good grades and participated in all sorts of extracurricular activities. I was sports editor for the school paper and captain of just about every team I ever played on.

My older brother Marvin had been captain of his team and a stand-out player at Wilby High School many years before. I was actually too young to go to many of the games but listened avidly on the radio. I knew every high school player in his league. To this day I can still recite the starting lineups for all his opposing teams.

My brother had always worn ankle weights when he was running for training. I decided to go him one better. I wore a twenty-pound weighted jacket as well. By the end of my basketball career at Sacred Heart, I had set records for most points in a season (604) and highest scoring average (28.8 points a game). To our disappointment, Sacred Heart did not win another state championship as we had the year before I came. But we did win three city championships, and I was elected all-state and all–New England and received some mention for high school all-American.

Just as important, however, were my academics. In fact, one of my most memorable confrontations at Sacred Heart took place over a grade I thought I deserved. It was my first semester. I was fourteen years old. We got our first report card back and I got 90 or above in every subject except religious studies. Sister Marian Joseph, my teacher, had given me an 89. I thought I deserved a higher grade. I told my mother and she encouraged me. "You're never going to get anything in life if you don't ask," she said. "Go in there and tell her you think you deserve a better grade."

I decided to do just that. I knew the minute I walked in the door that Sister wasn't used to this type of thing. There was a look of surprise on her face. Still, she kept smiling—a smile she always seemed to have even when she was telling you bad news.

I went straight to the point. "Sister, I wanted to ask you why I received a B in your course."

"Well, it's only the first marking period," she said. "You'll have a chance to bring that grade up."

"Yes, but Sister, all my other grades were A's. I got over ninety in every subject. I wanted to get straight A's my first marking period at Sacred Heart and you've given me a B."

"You got what you deserved based on what you did in class," she countered.

"I really disagree with you, Sister. I can show you my test scores. My average was around ninety-two or ninety-three, but you gave me an eighty-nine."

"That may be true on paper," she said, speaking very rapidly. "But you're forgetting that I take into consideration class participation."

"Class participation?" I couldn't figure out what she meant.

"Your hand is not up when I ask questions as frequently as others', so you lost points for that."

I tried to remember a time when my hand wasn't up. "Sister, my hand is up in class as frequently as anyone else's, as far as I can tell."

"Well, you may think so," she said, smiling, "but it's not. That's why I took a few points off your grade. Don't think this situation can't improve," she went on. "Obviously, this is only the first marking period. You have every chance to bring that grade up to an A and I feel confident you will do so."

Realizing I wasn't getting anywhere, I left. But I was determined I was not going to allow something I perceived as unfair to happen without letting the person in charge know about it—even if she was a nun. It was truly a lesson in objective and subjective evaluation.

From that day on, my hand was up in class at every opportunity. Every week or so I would say to her, "Sister, did you notice my hand? Did you see I had my hand up today? Did you see how many questions I answered?" That first marking period was the only time I ever received anything less than an A in her class.

At the end of my junior year, something happened that was to have a profound effect on the rest of my life. I ran for senior class president. My opponent, Tony Bergin, was the son of Edward Bergin, mayor of Waterbury. It was a foregone conclusion that he would win. The Bergins were a prominent family, and it was widely assumed that Tony himself might one day be mayor. (As it turned out, his brother, Edward Jr., made it instead.)

It wasn't a very promising campaign. Sacred Heart had four blacks in the entire student body of one thousand. But I knew then that white people would vote for a black person. When the ballots were counted, I won the election—to my own surprise more than anyone else's.

That got me thinking. "Gee, politics is fun," I said to myself. "I like getting up in front of people and debating. I think I might even like to do this when I grow up." It didn't happen all at once, but that election planted a seed in my mind. I was still thinking about it when it came time to choose a college.

Because of my basketball record, I was recruited by several schools throughout the country. At one point, I received a letter from William and Mary telling me they were sorry but I had been rejected for admission. This was surprising because I had never even applied to that school. Somebody in the athletic department had apparently recommended me as a potential candidate without my knowledge.

There were many basketball powerhouses that offered attractive athletic scholarships. Georgetown was one. But I decided at the beginning that I wanted to go to school on an academic scholarship. My favorite basketball player of the era was Dave Bing, a Syracuse University star whose style I often tried to imitate. But another favorite was Bill Bradley, a great Midwestern high school player who had gone to Princeton even though it did not have an outstanding basketball program. Bradley led Princeton to the NCAA Final Four and went on to play on two NBA championship teams with the New York Knicks. Although he could have gone to any basketball powerhouse in the country, he chose an Ivy League school. That's what I wanted to do, too.

Ivy League schools do not offer athletic scholarships, so I would have to go on an academic scholarship. My guidance counselor and several nay-saying nuns thought I wasn't Ivy League material. I persisted, though, and I received an offer for early admission from Dartmouth. I would have to accept it right away in order to go there, but my heart was set on Yale. For anyone growing up in the Nutmeg State, Yale University is the most prestigious school you can attend. If you're thinking about going to work in Connecticut, a degree from Harvard or Dartmouth just doesn't cut it. A Yale degree would be a plus for politics as well.

It was a tense wait, but in April 1971, I finally received the envelope from the Yale admissions office. Inside was a letter saying I had been accepted as a member of the Class of 1975. It was a dream that had once seemed beyond my reach.

I left Sacred Heart with intense feelings of gratitude and great hopes for the future. The school had given me a great education, plus the opportunity to participate and excel at a number of sports and activities. Father Blanchfield had truly been a second father to me, watching over me every step of the way.

Yet I also knew that I would now be entering a world that was beyond anything I had ever experienced or maybe even beyond my imagination. It was a world in which even the priests and nuns who had guided my education might themselves feel a little out of place. It was with a great deal of exhilaration—and not a little anxiety—that I prepared to go to Yale in the fall.

FOUR

~~~

Leaders among Leaders: My Life at Yale

M Y TWO ROOMMATES for my freshman year were Rick Andre, from Chicago, Illinois, and Greg Beams, from Xenia, Ohio. One of our funniest moments occurred on the first day, when our parents all came to drop us off and meet one another. After we got acquainted, we went down to the dining room for lunch. A lady at the front desk was checking identification cards. As we walked up to her, Greg said, "Beams," and I said, "Franks."

"Beans and franks? Hey, wait a minute, you two, come back here!"

"Those are our names, Beams and Franks," we said, innocently. "We're roommates." People around us began to titter.

She looked skeptically at our IDs. "Well, look at this—Beams and Franks. I thought you were playing a joke on me. And you two guys are roommates? Wouldn't you know it." By that time everyone on line was enjoying a good laugh.

That evening, we heard President Kingman Brewster give the freshmen a welcoming address. "You are one of a thousand individuals who will truly make a difference in this country," he told us. "You are leaders among leaders, having been selected to go to Yale, and it will become your responsibility to help lead this nation in the future." Granted, it was a bit of propaganda for Yale, but it was also very flattering for an eighteen-year-old.

Though I believed my mother's advice that "school is school," it became obvious pretty early that Yale was a place where the preppies—people who attended private boarding schools—had some advantage over people like me who had attended public or Catholic high schools. The prep school kids just seemed better prepared for the academic and social rigors of college life. They were used to living away from home.

Of course, this wasn't always such a great thing. I remember sitting around Farnham Hall one night and watching my next-door neighbors, three preppies from Phillips Exeter Academy, play a joke on their roommate by filling his room entirely with crumpled-up newspapers. It was supposed to teach him a lesson about cleanliness or something. I remember looking at the eight-by-ten room completely stuffed with wadded newspaper and wondering what would happen if somebody accidentally dropped a match. I was glad I hadn't gone to a place where that sort of thing was considered fun.

One of my first courses quickly taught me how different college was going to be. I remember taking copious notes and listening to everything the teacher had to say in preparation for the first test. When we got our first blue book, my mouth watered. I looked at the exam and saw it was everything I had studied. I wrote the answers to the three questions, thinking, "Boy, this is easy." When I turned my blue book in, I was surprised to realize that 90 percent of the class was still working on the test. "I must have it all over these guys," I remember thinking to myself.

As we waited to get our tests back the following week, I was absolutely positive I had gotten an A. When the teacher handed back the blue books, I walked slowly back to my seat, savoring the moment. I opened it slowly. There, in big red letters, the teacher had written: "I KNOW WHAT I SAID. WHAT DO YOU THINK?" My grade was a C.

It was a valuable awakening. I realized that Yale did not simply want you to absorb ideas but to think about them and challenge them as well. In order to stand up to the teacher, of course, you had to do your research and substantiate your point of view. But you could never let any idea go unexamined. It forced me to explore things from every possible angle, looking for aspects that might not be obvious at first but were helpful in developing a dialogue on an issue.

The other thing that impressed me at Yale was how hard everybody worked. At night when I would go to the library it was hard to find a place to sit down. Reading desk after reading desk was filled with students intensely poring over their homework. Whenever anybody tells me that getting into an Ivy League school gives you an easy time in life or means that you've got it made, I remind them of all the work it takes to get *through* one of those institutions. In my whole life, I don't think I've ever encountered people working harder than I did at college.

I met quite a number of other African Americans at Yale. It was a significant increase over my high school days. We had similar backgrounds, but I couldn't help noticing how many of them had parents and grandparents who had also attended college. As the son of working-class parents from a distinctly working-class town, I felt a bit different. This didn't become obvious to me until I began participating in the Black Students Alliance at Yale.

Since Yale was the sort of place where you could go all day without seeing another black person, many of us gravitated toward BSAY just out of habit. Most of our functions were social, but some were political. The general tone of these sessions was that Democrats were all good and Republicans were all bad. Everyone had complete disdain for anyone who wanted to be bourgeois. This puzzled me because most of my fellow BSAY members were much more bourgeois than I was. A few came from what could be called distinctly privileged backgrounds. I noticed the same thing tended to be true among white students who were involved in politics. It often seemed as if the more secure and comfortable you were in your background, the more far-left your political leanings were likely to be.

Like everyone else, I was a registered Democrat. I certainly didn't feel much in common with the Republicans—especially at a time when President Richard Nixon was in disgrace and the

Republicans were at a low ebb. But I knew I didn't feel entirely comfortable with the prevailing political winds that circulated through the campus either.

To me, what you accomplish seemed far more important than what you profess. One of the best experiences I had at Yale was teaching English at a local prison. I don't know why, but my grades started improving immediately. My father always said the more you give, the more you get. I guess that was applicable.

My one experience where I felt I was treated badly because of my race at Yale, surprisingly, took place on the basketball court. About three or four black players were making the team every year and Coach Joe Vancisin apparently didn't like it. In my first year, John Sherrill, one of the older players, told me that Coach Vancisin had a history of making blacks so upset and disgruntled that they ultimately never graduated from Yale. Quite specifically, it was said that he liked to "break niggers." During my stay at Yale, at least five black players fell prey to his manipulations. They would stay with the team for half a season or so and then quit in disgust. One player I helped recruit—a young man from Chicago named Mel Reynolds — left Yale a broken individual. Remarkably, I was to meet Mel Reynolds in very different circumstances many years later when we both sat in the Congressional Black Caucus.

In those days, freshmen could not play varsity sports but had their own program. I was captain of the frosh team and averaged twenty-five points a game. Although Yale was a perennial also-ran in Ivy League basketball, our freshman team offered hope for the future. It looked as if we might be able to perk up Yale basketball. During my sophomore year, Mel Reynolds was a rising star. He had transferred from a junior college, where he was an all-American. Soon Reynolds began to run into trouble with Coach Vancisin, however, and I was held up as the "good nigger"—the example of what a black player ought to be like. I felt a little uneasy. Some of Coach Vancisin's older victims started asking me how I tolerated him. For awhile, I wasn't sure what they were talking about. They would shake their heads and say, "Don't worry, the day will come when you will become the 'bad nigger.'"

One of my most vivid memories of college basketball was on a long bus ride back from Cornell two years later. As we rode home, someone announced that Mel Reynolds had just won a Rhodes Scholarship while at the University of Illinois. The black members on the team were overjoyed. We celebrated loudly enough so that Coach Vancisin, sitting at the front of the bus, clearly knew what we were whooping it up about. Mel later went on to serve with me in the U.S. House of Representatives. (He was forced to resign in 1995 after being convicted on charges of statutory rape.)

That was the first, though not the last, time that I saw someone play one black off against another in this "good black/bad black" fashion. Coach Vancisin seemed to suggest that these other players just lacked some mysterious ingredient that I had. Since then I have seen the same strategy used over and over to keep blacks in our place. There is always one black around they can hold up as a good example. Yet the same tactics will quickly be turned on the good black as soon as another comes along to take his place. When you're the one being treated well, you buy into the message that the other guy is no good and his "failure" is his own fault.

Only in my junior year did it become clear that I wasn't going to be a "good nigger" forever. My playing time went steadily downward. I scored 9.1 points per game as a sophomore, 6.8 as a junior, and 7.8 as a senior. In my senior year, I was elected captain of the team by the other players. Yet I still spent most of my time on the bench. After my spectacular freshman year, I had a disappointing career statistically.

Despite all this, I never quit. I persevered, worked hard, and prayed even harder for just one opportunity to show my talents. That chance finally came. As it turned out, it also became Coach Vancisin's last hurrah—although none of us realized it at the time.

Our last two home games at the Payne Whitney Gymnasium were against Dartmouth and Harvard, two teams that usually rank around third and fourth in the Ivy League, behind Princeton and Penn. As we huddled in the locker room before the Dartmouth game, Coach Vancisin announced that, in honor of our closing careers, the two seniors—me and another white player—would start the game. It was my big chance—but I was not as prepared as I thought I would be.

As I started running up and down the floor, I realized I was as rusty as a beached tugboat. Sitting on the bench for so long, I had lost my confidence; I didn't believe in myself. I tried to work out the kinks, but when the game started I performed badly, to the point of embarrassment. I could see Coach Vancisin sitting on the sidelines with a big smile on his face as I sputtered around the court. I imagined him saying, "You see, I knew this guy couldn't play." After a few more minutes of frustration, I was taken out. For the rest of the night, I sat and watched the Yale Bulldogs fall to the Dartmouth Indians.

I had truly lost faith in myself. I was afraid. I kept saying to myself, "Please, God, don't let Coach win this one. Don't let him win." But for that night, Coach Vancisin prevailed.

When I went home, I prayed and read the Bible for over an hour. During my visit to church the next day, I meditated twice as long as usual. Opportunities sometimes come only once in life. From that day forth, I decided that "Prepare, perform, and believe in yourself" would be my motto.

Our game that night was with Harvard. After church, I went down to the gym and shot baskets until I could hit from anywhere on the floor. When Coach Vancisin announced again that the seniors would start—with a special warning that we would be benched quickly if we didn't produce—I was ready.

That night I scored twenty-nine points, the high for any Yale player that season. The fans went crazy as I finally played up to the standards I had set as a freshman. A stunned Vancisin stood openmouthed on the sidelines. The two black players on the bench, Tim McChristian and Cornell Cooper, were beside themselves with elation as I continued to pour it on. The following week, as the result of my performance, I earned a spot on the weekly Eastern Collegiate Athletic Conference all-star team.

Of course I was thrilled, but I wanted to do even better. Our last two games were at Penn and Princeton, the two powerhouses of the Ivy League. Penn was headed for the NCAA national basketball tournament after being ranked in the top ten nationally. Princeton eventually won New York's National Invitation Tournament—the first Ivy League team ever to do so. After watching me score twenty-nine points against Harvard, Coach Vancisin was obligated to start me again. We played before a packed house at the Palestra in Philadelphia. Although we lost again, I performed well, scoring twenty points.

Now people were starting to ask why I hadn't been playing all year. Our team had compiled the second worst record in Yale basketball history, yet here I was scoring nearly twenty-five points a game after a whole year of sitting on the sidelines. Two of the white players actually went to *Yale* magazine to complain. When *Yale* interviewed me, I told them we had the talent to have a good team—it was just that Coach Vancisin did not get the most out of his players. When the story appeared a few weeks later, it proved to be Coach Vancisin's downfall. But all that didn't happen until the season was over.

My last game felt like a final examination in college hoops. The Princeton Tigers had one of the best defenses in the country, led by Armand Hill, a high school all-American who went on to play several years in the NBA. I scored twenty-four points, the most by any player against the Princeton defense all year. We lost again, but I felt I had passed. I proved to everyone I could have been a much better player—and we could have had a much better team—if Coach Vancisin had not been so rigid.

My last game turned out to be Coach Vancisin's last game as well. A few months after our season ended, he was forced to resign. The article in *Yale* magazine was the final nail in his coffin. My comments in that article—plus the obvious way he had kept me and others below our potential—played a big part in the outcome.

Perhaps one of the most memorable moments of my college career came when I was asked to join one of Yale's senior honor societies. One day I turned a corner on campus and found sixteen members standing in front of me. They went through their ritual of asking me to become part of the organization.

I said no. The sixteen members looked at me and one another as if I must be crazy. It was the most prestigious organization on campus—although I did not realize this until years later. Instead, I had a couple of good friends in another honor society, so I chose that instead. Many Yale alumni still can't believe I turned down the number one group, but I was happy with my choice. In fact, I still believe mine was the best.

Every Thursday night we would have a formal dinner. This was particularly interesting for me, since we rarely had formal dinners in my home other than at Thanksgiving and Christmas. Formal dinners with wine and cheese are not something to which a citizen of inner-city Waterbury is accustomed.

After dinner, we would sit around and talk about various subjects of the day. Each week one individual would also tell everyone about himself. We talked about our backgrounds, our ambitions, our experience at Yale, our plans for the future. Then everyone would ask questions and exchange comments. We developed a bond that I still maintain with several of my fellow members.

I left Yale feeling I had stored enough memories for a lifetime. I had done well in my studies. My basketball career—although disappointing—had at least cleared the way for other black players at Yale. I had friends and acquaintances from circles that I never could have imagined while growing up in Waterbury. Yet I felt strongly that I was the same person and hadn't abandoned my roots. I still believed that "prepare, believe in yourself, and perform" are the keys to success.

With all that in mind, I started looking for a job and a career.

FIVE

Finance and the Fortune 500

I HAD PLANNED TO go to graduate school after leaving Yale. However, I changed my plans when I got an invitation to try out for the New Orleans Jazz in the National Basketball Association. Butch van Breda Kolff, who became the color commentator for Princeton after coaching Bill Bradley's team there, had just been appointed the new coach of the Jazz. He had seen my performance against Princeton's Armand Hill. Although Coach Vancisin had thought I wasn't good enough to help Yale, Coach van Breda Kolff thought I might be able to help his new team and be paid for doing so.

At the time, the Jazz was led by Pistol Pete Maravich, a perennial all-star, and was about to get Gail Goodrich (often called Stumpy), a small (six-foot-one) guard who made the basketball Hall of Fame in 1996. I figured they thought I could fit in somewhere as a backup guard. It was also an honor to be attending a camp that would be partly supervised by Elgin Baylor, the great star of the 1960s and one of my idols, who was now on the Jazz's coaching staff.

At the time, I was engaged to Pamela Seaton, a Vassar undergraduate whom I had met my junior year at Yale. She lived in New Orleans and I stayed with her parents during the three-day tryout.

It was a grueling camp, filled with fine young players from across the country, all harboring the same ambition—catching on with an NBA team even though we had not been picked in the annual draft of college players. All we did was scrimmage up and down the court all day. It was an eerie feeling to watch Pistol Pete and some of the other Jazz starters exchanging comments on the sidelines and gesturing toward different players as they looked over the new crop of rookies.

We started with thirty players. By the last day we were down to ten and I was still among them. When Elgin Baylor and the other coaches made the final cut on the third day, however, I was eliminated. They asked us to try out for the Continental Basketball League, the minor league of the NBA, but I had had enough. I wouldn't be telling the truth if I said I wasn't disappointed, but I was ready to move on. Realizing that my basketball career was over, I went back to Connecticut. I decided to take some time off. I thought about going to law school. In the late spring I ended my hiatus and started looking for a job.

Yale helps its graduates obtain jobs, and in the middle of 1976, I landed a position with the Continental Can Company. I had other offers but was attracted to Continental because they said I could work and go to law school at night. I still had politics in the back of my mind. When I started work right after July 4, 1976, I made a vow that I would work ten years in the private sector before starting to explore the possibilities of working in my own business.

My first job was as a management trainee. Like many African Americans of that period, however, I quickly found myself being shunted into the personnel department. Although the job often went under other names, such as labor relations, employee relations, industrial relations, or human resources, I was essentially the old-time personnel officer dealing with a large number of people. Continental employed tens of thousands of workers all over the country and there was plenty to do. It gave me only a glimpse of the problems of running a large corporation.

My first boss was Bill Boozer, a fine Southern gentleman who truly wanted me to succeed if for no other reason than because he had taken a gamble, according to him, in hiring me. Some gamble. He had me interviewed by nine other people in one day before making his decision. That way a lot of other people were on the hook if it didn't work out.

When I first started, I was a chronic procrastinator. My work often went unsupervised and I had trouble getting my job done. Boozer sat me down in his office and told me that he didn't want to terminate me, but if I didn't improve I might not be around for long. He taught me a basic organizational tool: put together a list each day of things you think you can accomplish. At the end of the day, you should have them finished. I followed the routine day after day, week after week. Before long, I found myself getting everything done. Often I finished my list early. That gave me time to do things above and beyond the call of duty, as Boozer would say. I would plan longer-term projects and expand my horizons. After a while, these things began to impress my superiors.

Although Boozer had put me in fear of losing my job, I had turned things around so that I was now excelling. After a few months, I was promoted to Reading, Pennsylvania, where I became the top personnel staffer at a 350-man plant in Continental's fiber drum division.

The lessons Boozer taught me—discipline, persistence, and the "cover your derriere" value of maintaining a paper trail—truly gave me the equivalent of an on-the-job M.B.A. Many of the people I worked with at Continental, however, had real M.B.A.'s or law degrees or other postgraduate credentials. As someone with only a bachelor's degree, I was pleased to be able to compete with them.

There were tensions, especially related to race. I remember feeling very awkward during the time when ABC was airing the epic series *Roots* on television. Like the rest of the country, our office became wrapped up in this gripping narrative. It seemed as if everyone wanted to talk about the program, but no one wanted to be the first one to bring it up. My coworkers might have felt more comfortable if I had been the one to initiate the discussion, but I didn't feel it was my place to broach the subject. So no one did.

I also recall speaking with one of our plant managers by phone several times before paying him a visit at our plant in Mississippi. The day before I set off, he asked me, "Do you know where you're headed tomorrow?"

"Jackson, Mississippi, of course."

"You're coming into the heart of Dixie," he continued. "Oh, by the way, as far as I'm concerned I like you, but I think you've got three strikes against you."

"What do you mean, three strikes?" I wondered.

"Number one, you're black. Number two, you went to Yale. Number three, I hear you have a beard." Maybe he was just being facetious, but his comments made me feel a little bit concerned about visiting a small town in the Deep South.

Lo and behold, the trip turned out to be a very pleasant one. I was down there primarily to discuss the plants' affirmative action plan. Everything went smoothly and the trip itself was completely copacetic.

One other memorable brush with bigotry came without my ever leaving the North. During my first few months I was working in Philadelphia as a trainee in Continental's industrial relations department. One evening, I went to dinner with my manager at a local Marriott Hotel restaurant to get better acquainted, since we had only worked together for a week or two. When dinner was over, he grabbed the check. When he opened his wallet, I got a glimpse of an ID card he carried. It read KNIGHTS OF THE KLAN right across the top. He quickly tried to cover it, but when he looked at me he realized I had seen it. "I don't know why I still have this in my wallet," he stammered with embarrassment. "I'm not even a part of that group anymore." How comforting.

Having had a father and several cousins who worked as blue-collar laborers—and having done factory work myself during a few of my summers at Yale—it was interesting for me to see the industrial environment from the management perspective. Quite frankly, it was a real disappointment to see how many of the supposed confrontations between labor and management were little more than a game of charades.

One of my early responsibilities was to be an information specialist during labor negotiations. I would have to research all the possible issues we might fight over. For example, if the union representative wanted the company to pay for shoes and uniforms because XYZ company did, the chief negotiator would look down the table at me for a response. I would tell him that XYZ company does indeed supply its employees with shoes and uniforms but most of the other companies in our field do not.

What I soon learned was that these formal negotiations—usually accompanied by a lot of breast-beating rhetoric—were often just for show. Several times I accompanied my boss to a secret rendezvous with the union representative during which they would go over in a very civilized manner exactly how far each side was willing to go. In front of other people, it was different. The union guy would give us hell. He had to maintain the fiction that the company was the bad guy and the union was the good guy and the only way the workers would ever get anything was by sticking with the union. As my boss used to say, "After every negotiation, the union has to feel that they raped us while really we raped them."

The union rep's real concern was that he didn't want to go back to a line job. He much preferred walking around in a white collar, negotiating contracts and handling grievances all day. At my second job in Reading, I found things didn't have to be this way. As the personnel officer there, I set up dances, Christmas parties, and a number of activities that brought labor and management together socially. The result was a more cohesive and productive organization.

After a year and a half at Continental Can, I decided to broaden my horizons. In January 1978, I accepted a position at Chesebrough-Pond's, makers of Pond's cold cream and many other health and beauty products. I was appointed assistant manager for corporate recruitment. At twenty-four, I was one of the youngest managers in the company. I was making 50 percent more than I had made at Continental and was able to buy my first property, a condo in Stamford, Connecticut.

At Chesebrough-Pond's, I was involved in about two-thirds of the corporate hiring. Because I was recruiting for every department in the company, I got a real feel for what the business was about. I worked with the departments of market research, taxes, accounting, sales, marketing, product management, and labor relations.

I also had responsibility for affirmative action. Far from

involving quotas and other divisive standards, affirmative action, as we practiced it, simply meant broadening the spectrum of candidates from which we chose new employees. Many employers—even some of the largest corporations in the country—still operate on the "father-son" principle or draw their employees from "friends of friends." People create networks, and friends and relatives still get a surprising amount of preference. It was my job to broaden these old networks to include people outside the normal channels—including a lot of minorities. I became very proud of my efforts. It didn't bother me at all to tell one of the managers, "No, we are not going to hire your friend," or "No, we are not going to hire your son. We'll just put his résumé in a pile with all the others and hire the best person for the job."

Unfortunately, my employment at Chesebrough-Pond's came to an abrupt end because of office politics. Our supervisor in the personnel department was not doing her job well. Just about everybody working for her was dissatisfied. She was allowing a personal problem to affect her job. Instead of seeking professional help, she took out her frustrations on her staff. Three of us got together and decided to approach the vice president of personnel. I was elected to be our spokesperson. During the meeting, I had the distinct impression that, although the vice president was pleased that I was willing to take on the responsibility, he also felt I was being disloyal. (He happened to be a close friend of the problem employee.) As a result of our efforts, the supervisor was terminated. But shortly after, I was laid off as well. I always thought it was because of the way I handled the situation, although it may have been nothing more than corporate downsizing. After setting up severance packages for so many other employees, I found myself on the receiving end.

I received several months' pay. For awhile, I tried sitting around the house catching up on personal projects, but the days seemed thirty-six hours long. Well before my severance was up, I had another job at Peter Paul Cadbury, a division of Cadbury Schweppes PLC, which has been manufacturing candies in Naugatuck, south of Waterbury, for more than seventy-five years. This allowed me to help care for my ailing father, slowly start my real estate business, and also begin dabbling in politics.

At Cadbury Schweppes, I was soon in charge of human resources for plants throughout the country. I reported to the vice president for human resources for North America. One of my most difficult assignments was relocating a large group of individuals from our Naugatuck facility down to the company headquarters in Stamford. I performed so well that the company gave me a car as a bonus. I also became good friends with Jim Schadt, the president of Cadbury Schweppes and now president of *Reader's Digest*. To this day he remains a personal friend and one of my strongest financial contributors.

Still, when the magic date of July 4, 1986, rolled around, I thought I had done enough. I had been working for *Fortune* 500 companies for exactly ten years. It had taught me to handle challenges and shaped me as a professional. I had learned much about large organizations. But I was ready for something different. I wanted to try my hand as a full-time entrepreneur.

I began managing my father's old three-decker and buying other buildings until I owned more than a dozen properties around Connecticut, including several in white neighborhoods. I also built a few homes. Here again, my race became a problem. The first question prospective tenants always seemed to ask was whether I owned the building. When I told them I did, their attitude changed considerably. Some people probably thought I seemed a bit young to be a real estate magnate. If the prospective tenants were my age, they often seemed a little envious. Most of all, they didn't seem to like the idea of putting money in a black man's pocket.

I began refusing to answer the question. I told people the building was owned by a group of people—which in fact included only one of my sisters and myself. Sometimes it got so bad I simply told people I was the managing agent. That seemed to make them feel better. In many instances, they took the apartment right away. But whenever prospective renters saw me as the owner of the building, it soured the interview. I lost a lot of good tenants this way.

Almost unwittingly, I became involved with politics. In the summer of 1982, a water main broke at our old three-decker on Camp Terrace. We asked the city government to fix it, but they argued that it was our responsibility because the street was not on the official town map. The mayor was none other than Edward Bergin Jr., son of the former mayor and brother of my opponent for senior class president at Sacred Heart.

The city government fixed up a hose from a neighboring supply of water to service the three-decker. We waited for the mayor to do more. Nothing happened. Fall rolled around and we began to worry that the hose would freeze, leaving my tenants without water. The papers picked up the story and before long I was on a radio show airing my complaints. The TV stations were just starting to call when the mayor relented and repaired the pipe.

At the time I was also serving on the boards of many community organizations: the YMCA, the Boys' Club, the Red Cross, and the Opportunities Industrialization Center, a local group trying to bring jobs into depressed areas. I was usually very vocal at these meetings about one thing and another, and people would often come up and say, "You know, you ought to go into politics."

Then one day I paid a visit to a local insurance broker who was carrying the policy on one of my buildings. It was a routine visit, but it changed my life.

SIX

Entering Politics:
Franks for Alderman

IN November 1983, I walked into the Waterbury offices of Martin and Rowland Insurance to renew a policy on one of my buildings. For many years, my father had done business with Sherwood Rowland, the senior partner. In recent years, he had turned over much of the business to his sons. One of them, John, was emerging as a wonder boy of Connecticut politics.

Four years younger than I, John had already been elected to the state legislature in 1980 at the age of twenty-three. He was now rumored to be preparing for a run for Congress. As I entered, John sat with his sleeves rolled up in an open bull pen surrounded by five empty desks, while his father, Sherwood, sat in an enclosed glass office.

I had nothing in mind that day other than renewing my insurance policy. But Rowland had followed my basketball career and knew of the water main incident. The talk soon turned to other things.

"Gary, is it true you're thinking about getting involved in politics?" John asked.

"I guess I've given it some thought," I said, trying to sound non-committal. The Waterbury Republicans had just suffered another dismal defeat. Mayor Bergin had been reelected again and the Democrats had a majority on the fifteen-member board of aldermen. I knew they were looking for new blood.

"We are looking at trying to take over the town committee in Waterbury this year," he said. "I know what you're thinking. Right now the Republicans in this town could hold their meetings in a phone booth. But we're going to change things. The party's infra-structure is old and needs to be cleaned out. We're going to put together a coalition that can move us forward. I think you can be part of it."

I thanked him and said I'd give it some thought.

"I won't try to hide my own interest in this thing," he added. "I'm planning to run for Congress next year. I'll need a strong Waterbury Republican Party behind me."

John made it to Congress in 1984, serving for three terms in the seat I would eventually hold. In 1994, he was elected gov-ernor of Connecticut.

A few weeks later, I walked into my first Republican leaders' meeting. It was held at the home of Charlie Messer, a chain-smoking businessman whose company would eventually win a six-figure car-towing contract from the city government.

As I entered the powwow, I recognized only a few people. Some I had seen at town meetings or read about in the newspaper. About thirty of us sat on a long bench that was literally carved into the walls of Charlie's basement. At the head table sat Perry Piscotti, a three-hundred-pound training executive at 7-Eleven who served as town chairman. To his right was Fran Donnarumma, Rowland's campaign manager. On the other side sat Don Schmidt, one of the few non-Italians in the group.

What struck me immediately was that we were sitting in almost total darkness. It was as if the cliché had come to life. I felt as if I was sitting in one of those legendary smoke-filled rooms where all important political decisions are supposedly made.

Perry Piscotti called the meeting to order by apologizing for the party's crushing defeat in November. He offered to step aside if that would help change the party's image in the public eye. "We've got to assemble a new team," he said, nodding at Schmidt, who had only recently been recruited. "We've got to open the party to people from different backgrounds and ethnic groups. I may be the old guard," he concluded, "but I also want to be part of the new guard."

As part of the new guard, I was nominated for a seat on the town committee. We were attempting to oust the "old guard." That meant I had to run for election. It was a difficult race since I knew few registered Republicans—and even fewer Republicans of color. But I did my best, knocking on doors and speaking at small groups. On Election Day I won the fifth of five seats on the committee by fewer than a dozen votes.

Our new group captured four of the five state representative districts, giving us effective control of the town committee. Perry Piscotti kept his promise by stepping down as chairman and turning the gavel over to Don Schmidt. Piscotti remained active in the background, however, and effectively ran the Waterbury GOP. When the elections of 1985 rolled around, we were ready to put up our reformed slate.

A number of people wanted Fran Donnarumma to be our candidate for mayor, since he was a prominent attorney. But the old guard prevailed and the nod went to Joe Santopietro, a young blue-collar worker who operated his own lawn-care business. I told the committee that I would like to run for the board of aldermen. In keeping with their vow to broaden the party, they agreed to put me on the slate.

Aldermanic races in Waterbury have a peculiar format, easily manipulated by local politicians. Candidates for all fifteen seats run at large. However, each party is allowed to put up only nine candidates, and each voter casts ballots for only nine candidates. The result is that the minority party is assured at least six seats on the board.

A more important oddity is that candidates are paired against each other in alphabetical order. Although voters are told over and over that they can vote for both candidates on the same line, people still tend to believe they must choose between opponents who are listed next to each other. As a result, being listed against a popular candidate is a big handicap. By chance or design, I was paired against Bill Monti, the biggest vote-getter in Waterbury. No Republican running opposite Monti had ever won. Few people thought I could do well and not many gave Joe Santopietro much of a chance either.

I began my campaign by sending out letters reminding people that I grew up in the area, had worked for three *Fortune* 500–type companies, and was on the board of directors of the local Red Cross, YMCA, and Boys' Club. I even raised money for radio advertisements. Then I got an idea.

During the campaign, I had made several comments critical of Mayor Bergin. I had spoken on the stump of filling vacant lots with houses, bringing industry into the city, and trying to establish a four-year state college in Waterbury. The mayor had completely ignored us.

So I ran a radio ad that proposed these ideas, then added, "When asked to respond, Mayor Ed Bergin said . . ." Five seconds of dead air followed. "That's his answer for us," the spot continued, "but on Election Day, we'll have an answer for him. Vote for Alderman Joe Santopietro for mayor, Gary Franks for alderman, and the entire Republican team."

That ad helped ignite the Republican campaign. At the wrap-up rally before the election, several people told me they were sorry I had been paired against Monti because I had made a real contribution to the campaign. They urged me to try again in two years. Imagine everyone's surprise when I received the second-highest total in the entire city, surpassed only by longtime Republican incumbent Paul Vitarelli. The next morning, the citizens of Waterbury awoke to find they had elected twenty-six-year-old Joe Santopietro as mayor and given him a Republican majority on the board of aldermen.

Before we took control of the city government, I attended a number of organizational meetings. From the outset, I could sense something strange going on. Every time I walked into the room, the conversation would stop on a dime. At first I decided it was because I was black and people were uneasy in my presence. Then I began talking with Jack Donahue, an incumbent Republican alderman, and he said the same thing was happening to him. We began joking about it. Every time either of us walked into the room, the conversation stopped or someone scurried off to the men's room. Only years later did we find out the real story.

On January 1, 1986, we were sworn in. I was startled to learn that I had been selected president pro tempore of the board of aldermen and had been listed as vice chairman of the zoning commission and a commissioner of the fire board—three extremely influential positions. I asked Don Schmidt why I was being given so much responsibility. "They need to legitimize the new administration," he told me. "You don't realize it, but you're one of the linchpins of this administration. As a Yale graduate and former Sacred Heart basketball star, you're somebody the public feels comfortable with. You make the boys look good."

I knew I had my work cut out for myself. The zoning board promised to be particularly time-consuming since Waterbury was going through a building boom. As a fire commissioner, I would be involved in evaluating building codes, maintaining fire stations, and dealing with general response and safety. Yet I also saw them as opportunities. I worked with the fire and police departments to hire more blacks and Hispanics and have them promoted through the ranks. During my tenure, three blacks became police sergeants and one became a fire lieutenant.

At a private session just prior to our first board of aldermen's meeting, majority leader Bob Giacomi and board president Paul Vitarelli stressed that we had to stick together. We were new to power and we would have to strive to keep that majority, even if it meant that individuals would occasionally have to vote against their own inclinations. That did not sound good. I knew it wasn't going to work for me. The public did not expect to have robots in office.

The problems were on the zoning board. Developers were coming in constantly, asking for zoning changes to build condominiums. Many of these changes seemed ill-advised and were arousing considerable opposition from the people in their neighborhoods. Still, the Republican-dominated board rubber-stamped them one after another.

On several key votes I split with the Republican majority and sided with the two Democratic members. After one of these decisions, Perry Piscotti, who was in the audience, leaped out of his seat, stormed from the room, and slammed the door behind him. Later I heard the whole administration was furious with me. Even then, it never occurred to me that anything sinister might be going on.

Later that year I took my case to the public. I offered a new piece of legislation that would prohibit changing the zoning on a property without notifying the people in surrounding areas that would be affected by the decision. When I introduced these measures at the zoning commission, Republican chairman Steve Somma screamed that I was misleading the public. The story made the front page of the *Waterbury Republican.*

The people of Waterbury soon rallied around me. The ordinance was passed almost exactly as I had proposed—with Mayor Santopietro's name on it instead of mine. That didn't bother me a bit. The more important issue was that the citizens of Waterbury would no longer have to endure radical zoning changes in their neighborhoods without prior knowledge. Residents could present petitions that would force the zoning commission to approve the change by a two-thirds vote instead of a simple majority. The measure was immensely popular with the public and slowed the condominium mania considerably. People told me I ought to consider running for mayor.

In 1986, I again stood against the Republicans on the matter of constructing a grade school in Waterbury's predominantly Hispanic section. The Santopietro administration was trying to remodel an old supermarket into an elementary school. I argued that the Hispanic people of Waterbury deserved better. Only later did it emerge that members of the administration had a financial interest in the property—a revelation that eventually led to the arrests and convictions of Santopietro and his associates.

While the board of aldermen was debating a vote on the supermarket bond package, Bobby Giacomi and Paul Vitarelli approached me during the recess. "You might as well be a Democrat," Giacomi screamed at me. "You won't support anything we do!" I told him I couldn't do so in good conscience. He flung his arms in the air and stomped out of the caucus room.

The measure fell two votes short of the necessary two-thirds majority. I was one of the holdouts. As punishment for my independence, Vitarelli appointed me as a special committee of one to review the school matter and propose a better recommendation.

In addition to everything else, I discovered that several companies had dumped hazardous waste on the supermarket site. The story made the *Hartford Courant*. Eventually the city government voted to build a new school from the ground up—just as I had always insisted.

Toward the end of my first two-year term, Perry Piscotti invited me to have breakfast with him at Howard Johnson's. It sounded like a visit to the woodshed.

"Gary, a lot of people in the party feel you should be banished," Perry began. "You shouldn't be a Republican any longer—certainly not an elected official. People feel you have a great deal of talent but you're showing the type of disloyalty that is ultimately going to defeat us in the next election."

"Perry," I told him, "as far as I'm concerned, I'm going to do what I feel is right. If the party is right on an issue, I'll vote Republican. If it is clearly wrong, I will vote against the Republicans. If it's something in a gray area, I will stick with the party and give it the benefit of the doubt. That's all I can assure you."

Piscotti seemed to interpret this as a victory. "I believe you deserve another shot," he said. "I'm looking forward to working with you in the next election."

I knew it was going to be a tough one. The word on the street was that I was going to be dumped from the list of Republican candidates for office. A reporter from the *Waterbury Republican* even asked me to comment on the rumor that I was getting too big for my britches and the party was going to take me down a notch or two.

I got the nomination, however, and was paired against Nicholas Parillo, another very popular Democratic incumbent. Much of my opposition came from Republicans. They accused me of working against Mayor Santopietro and running a "bullet campaign" in which I only promoted myself without advancing the interests of the party.

When the votes came in, I once again finished near the top of the ticket. What votes I lost in the tightly disciplined Republican wards I made up by a growing strength in the black community.

After my victory, I knew I was going to be replaced as president pro tem of the board of aldermen. Sure enough, Paul Vitarelli told me the administration had made a mistake: the position should have gone to Jack Donahue, who was in line for it after the 1985 elections. As we were sworn in, I learned I would also be removed from the zoning commission and the fire board. Instead I would be serving on the Silas Bronson Library board and the Civil Service Commission—both nonvoting positions. I would not even be allowed to participate in debates. This was my punishment for not playing ball.

At the next aldermen's meeting, Mayor Santopietro swept past me on his way into the chamber. I found I had been moved from the front of the room to a seat in the back row. Both the mayor and Paul Vitarelli told reporters that it was being done because I had not been returning phone calls and I had not been conscientious about my work.

I took vigorous exception to these comments and took a half-page ad in the *Waterbury Republican* telling people of my hometown exactly why I was being blacklisted. I opposed rubber-stamp zoning changes and wanted the people of Waterbury to have their say. Thousands of my constituents responded positively to the ad with letters, phone calls, and backslaps on the street.

Still, my standing with the administration remained on tenterhooks. Stripped of all responsibilities, I resigned myself to living in the doghouse for the rest of my days in office. There didn't seem to be any way to improve my standing in Waterbury. Maybe the only way out would be to shoot for something higher.

SEVEN

"The Last Shall Be First..."

M Y WIFE, Donna, and I walked hand in hand down a dirt path at nearly four-thirty in the morning outside the Oxford Tavern in Oxford, Connecticut. We had just fled a sea of reporters, family members, friends, and fellow delegates. At about 3:30 A.M. the Connecticut State Republican Party had nominated me as its candidate for the Fifth Congressional District.

It still seemed unreal. As we strolled along, laughing and talking softly to each other, it was like a secret only we two shared. "God truly worked a miracle," I told her. Saying anything more might make it all vanish into thin air.

Then the spell was broken. Jon Lender, a reporter for the *Hartford Courant,* came running up to ask for an interview. He asked all the usual questions.

"I'll tell you one thing," said Lender, rushing off to meet his deadline. "You never cease to amaze people."

"It's like it says in the Bible," I shouted after him. "The last shall be first and the first shall be last."

How did it happen? Even in retrospect, it seems like a nearly impossible long shot. I had come into the convention the previous evening running dead last among five strong candidates. No one gave me the slightest chance. Yet after seven hours of intrigue, countermaneuvers, betrayals, and obvious divine intervention, each of my opponents had done himself in and I had emerged the winner.

It all began in 1986, right after my conflict with the Waterbury Republican Party emerged. Their feeling seemed to be that although I was useful to have around as a big vote-getter, the sooner I moved on to something else, the better. In July 1986, I was asked by State Senator Dick Bozzuto to run for state comp-troller after being an alderman for only six months. This sur-prised a lot of people. I lost, but led the entire state Republican ticket and carried the Fifth Congressional District. In 1987—this time at the urging of Congressman Rowland—I made a run for state party chairman. But my support deserted me at the state convention and the job went to Bob Poliner, who was the choice of Sen. Lowell Weicker.

So it was back to my strained position on the board of aldermen, where I again won by a big margin in 1989. Right after the election, I got another call from Perry Piscotti asking for yet another breakfast at Howard Johnson's.

"First, let me congratulate you on your victory," said Perry, struggling to steer his three hundred pounds into the narrow booth. "Once again you were our second-best vote-getter in the whole race."

"I'm happy about that but I'm even happier that the whole Republican ticket won," I said.

"You did a great job, Gary. You get the black vote. You do well in the Town Plot. What do you plan to do now?"

"I'm thinking of going to John Rowland and asking if I can have another shot at state comptroller," I said, digging into my eggs and toast. After serving in Congress for six years, Rowland was making his first run for governor—a race he would lose, although he would win on his second try in 1994.

"Gary," said Piscotti, taking a healthy bite of his English muffin, "I don't think John's going to need you. After all, you're both from the fifth district. He's going to have to balance his ticket."

"I almost won for comptroller in 1986. Don't you think I deserve another shot?"

Perry shook his head, working his jaws. "Why do you want to run for comptroller?" he asked when he had finally cleared his palate.

"I think I can win. It would be a big step in my political career.

Piscotti took a long sip of coffee. "Congress," he pronounced, finally coming back up for air.

"What do you mean, 'Congress'?"

"You should run for Congress."

"Isn't Santopietro going to run? He's following in Rowland's footsteps."

Perry leaned back in his chair, exhausted by his deglutitions. "It won't happen," he said. "I've known Joe a long time. He'd make a good congressman, but it's not going to happen."

"He hasn't said anything to me about it," I reflected.

"He won't," Perry said authoritatively. "Listen, Gary, you'd make a good congressman. You have brains. You're black. You're different. . . ." He struggled for a word. "Articulate."

"You think I could win in the Valley?" (where people say they'd never vote for a black person), I tested him.

"Don't concern yourself with that," he said, mopping up with his napkin. "You can win. Toby Moffett's going to be the Democratic candidate and you can beat him."

"You think it'll be Moffett over Pacowta?" Moffett was a former congressman from the state's northwest corner. Pacowta was the former mayor of Shelton, the district's fifth-largest town, and strong Republican territory.

"Yes, Moffett. He has it all. He's got money, recognition—you name it. He'll be the nominee. But you can take him. You can win this city," he said, jabbing his finger in the air. "And when you've got Waterbury, you've won the whole ball game." He swept his hands across the table, as if gathering up the map of the district.

"That's why Joe can't make it," he continued. "He can win in Waterbury, but lots of people in the western end of the district don't like Italians. You may not know this, but Rowland doesn't even send his own chief of staff, John Mastropietro, down there anymore. He sends an Irish guy, Frannie Brennan. They don't want to see Italians down there. Black? They'll like that. They'll go for a black guy, especially one from Yale. They may even forget you're from Waterbury."

Perry chuckled at his own wisdom. "I've heard some of the people down on the gold coast say they think it would be chic to vote for a black Yalie."

"Well, it's something to give some thought to."

"Well, you give it some thought," he said, rising. "But I think you'll see I'm right. We're behind you, Gary, if you decide to run."

I left Howard Johnson's with my belly full and my mind reeling.

A few days later I strolled into John Rowland's Waterbury office. The congressman was on the phone, trying, it seemed, to talk someone into making a campaign contribution. But since it's not proper to raise funds from congressional offices, I'm sure I got it wrong.

John hung up and called John Mastropietro into the meeting. Mastropietro and I had been classmates at Sacred Heart. I told both of them I wanted to run for state comptroller and was looking for their support. The phone rang before Rowland could even open his mouth; he excused himself and took it in another room.

Mastropietro began to tell me it would be difficult for Rowland to have a candidate from the fifth district. "He's got to spread things around the state," he said.

"But I think I could draw votes from everywhere."

Mastropietro switched gears. "Look, try raising fifty thousand dollars by April first. Then try to get some of your contributors to give to John's campaign. If you can tell us, 'This guy's going to help us raise X amount of money,' it might do the trick."

Rowland stayed on the phone so long that I eventually went home.

My next stop was Dick Foley, who had taken over for Bob Poliner as state chairman in 1989. I had to cool my heels outside his office quite a while before he finally came down. "How's it going?" he asked, skipping down the stairs. "I understand you want to run for state comptroller."

"Who told you that?"

"Oh, a little birdie," he said gleefully. "He pecked at my window and said, 'Franks for comptroller.'" Foley laughed and added, "What about Congress?"

"Everybody keeps pushing me for Congress."

Foley leaned closer. "I think you could upset the apple cart."

"Well, if Santopietro doesn't run, I'll think about it."

"He's going to decide in a couple of weeks," Foley confided. "They're doing a poll to see what his numbers look like. Look, it's January. You've got a number of candidates out there. But if Joe decides not to run, I think the boys are ready to help you." ("The boys," of course, were Mayor Santopietro's machine.)

"I don't know whether I need them. I'm already strong in Waterbury."

"Look," said Foley, lowering his voice again, "the boys can raise a lot of money for you. If Joe wanted to run, he could raise hundreds of thousands of dollars just like that"—snapping his fingers. "Keep in mind, he raised three hundred fifty thousand dollars for the mayoral campaign last year, when he got sixty-six percent of the vote. He's got Richard Barbieri raising money for him. Barbieri has people who can fork out a thousand dollars just like that. All of a sudden he's got fifty thousand dollars. The same thing can happen for you if you decide to run."

Richard Barbieri was president of Security Savings Bank, the region's fastest-growing savings and loan, and past finance chairman of Mayor Santopietro's previous campaigns. He was looked upon as being a wonder boy of finance while investors and members of his board of directors were known for becoming wealthy in a very short period of time.

"Perry told me the same thing," I remarked. "He said he could raise a good amount of money to get me started."

Foley shrugged. "Look, if you're ready to run, they're ready to back you."

I told him I'd give it some thought. If Mayor Joe really decided not to run I would give up my campaign for state comptroller and shoot for Congress.

By Mayor Joe's inaugural ball in mid-January, he still hadn't made up his mind. As a result, the black-tie affair was rife with intrigue. I brought Donna Williams, a woman I had met in real estate and who was soon to become my wife. It was her first political outing.

Almost the first person she noticed was Jamie McLaughlin,

state senator from Woodbury, who was openly pushing for the congressional nomination.

"Good to see you, Jamie," I said as he glad-handed us. "I see you had to come and kiss the mayor's ring," I added, referring to Santopietro.

"Oh, not yet," he laughed. "Waterbury should be my turf, unless Timmy gets in the race." (Tim Upson was another state senator.) "I don't think Alan Schlesinger or Warren Sarasin are very serious either." (Schlesinger was a representative from Derby; Sarasin was the younger brother of a former congressman.) "I figure if Joey drops out I've got a clear shot."

I hinted that I might be interested in running. McLaughlin looked vexed. "You think you might?" Then someone interrupted us and he tacked on one of those political smiles. "See you guys later."

"Politics is backstabbing with a smile," Donna commented.

A month later, Mayor Joe finally held his press conference. In front of four television cameras and a room full of reporters, he announced that, although he felt he could win the race for Congress, he wanted to stay in Waterbury and concentrate on improving the city.

"Actually, the boys decided there aren't as many jobs in a congressional office," Steve Beaujon, Mayor Joe's press secretary, confided to me later. "They think they can do better by staying in town."

By February, we had four candidates. They were McLaughlin, Schlesinger, Sarasin, and Steve Watson, a young Danbury novice and former aide to Lee Atwater, the Republican national chairman. Steve Beaujon began warning me I had better jump in soon. "We'll put out some leaks and generate some press coverage," he told me. "But you're starting out in last place. You'd better get your act together."

Fair enough. Before I threw my hat in, though, I went to Washington to see how much support the Republican National Committee was prepared to give me.

"We're working very hard to get black Republicans elected," said David Byrd, who was working with the minority outreach program. "Right now our big prospect is Ken Blackwell, a retired pro football player and former mayor of Cincinnati. We got him to switch parties."

"Are there any other black candidates around?"

"There's Al Brown, in Kentucky, but that's about it. I'm sorry we haven't been in touch with you, but you just haven't been on our radar screen."

I tried to fill him in a little on my background.

"Who's your likely opponent?"

"Toby Moffett, the former congressman."

"The one who worked for Ralph Nader?"

"That's right."

"He's got name recognition, doesn't he?"

"He's been a TV anchorman for the last few years. He's known all over the state."

"Well, you've got a rough road ahead of you. If you make up your mind, though, get in touch with us. We think it would be great if you run."

Nobody said a word about money. "A tremendous degree of comfort and encouragement," I thought wryly as I walked down the steps of the Dwight Eisenhower Republican National Center.

In late February, the National Republican Congressional Committee sent a representative to Connecticut to brief us on its plans. Although I still hadn't announced, Dick Foley told me I'd better be there.

As I walked into the Brookside Inn in Oxford, all eyes instantly shifted toward me. They probably hadn't seen a black patron in many moons. Jamie McLaughlin and Warren Sarasin were milling about with their entourages, while I only had Bob Keating, my part-time staffer.

"So what brings you here?" said Alan Schlesinger, bustling over with a sardonic smile.

"Take one guess, Alan."

"Oh-oh, another Waterbury candidate. I think we need more of you guys in the race."

Alan was happy to have as many Waterbury opponents as possible, since it would split the city's vote.

"So you're getting in, too?" asked Warren Sarasin, sipping on a soft drink.

"I guess I am," I said sheepishly. "I'll probably announce soon."

The NRCC representative, Dan Leonard, hammered one point home. We should pick a nominee at our convention and not spill blood in a September primary. If we didn't settle our differences internally, the NRCC would pull out. "Moffett's going to be very tough to beat and he can probably raise a million dollars," Leonard told us. "We hate to lose a seat we've already got. But if you people can't settle your differences at a convention, we're not going to be able to help you in the campaign."

Two weeks later I threw my hat in the ring. Unlike Mayor Santopietro's announcement *not* to run, which had drawn all the TV stations, my press conference drew only CableVision Norwalk. Two radio stations and a handful of reporters also showed up. Among my supporters were my mother; Donna; and my six-year-old soon-to-be stepdaughter, Azia.

I told the small gathering that I was running for Congress because, among other reasons, I wanted to make America even greater than it was. I spoke for about ten minutes. The reporters had few questions. That was it. Right after the news conference, Donna and I got our marriage license. We honeymooned for a week on St. Martin.

When we got back, my first campaign stop was Redding, a small suburban town on the district's gold coast near Long Island Sound. I addressed the Republican town committee. This was suburbia at its most fashionable. Jason Bartlett, my campaign assistant, and I were the only black people in the room. My knees were shaking. I couldn't tell what kind of impression I was making. But the group was friendly and receptive, more so than I had anticipated.

When the questions started, however, everyone wanted to know why I was getting in the race so late. "Why did you spend the last week on vacation?" someone asked.

"I was on my honeymoon," I said. "I only plan to have one."

Still, the mood was skeptical. When the meeting was over, I found the scuttlebutt was that I was just a stalking horse for Mayor Santopietro or some other Waterbury candidate. Politics is strange, I thought as we drove home. I went in there worrying about being a black man in a white crowd. I ended up being perceived as a blue-collar Italian trying to put one over on affluent suburbia.

The scene was repeated again and again at wine-and-cheese receptions, breakfasts, lunches, and dinners. "It's too bad you didn't get in earlier," people would say. Most admitted they were already committed to someone else. At one meeting, though, something dramatic happened. After I had finished speaking, a woman named Norma Riess stood up, pointed her finger at me, and announced, "You're going to be the candidate." Everyone in the room was stunned. It was as if a soothsayer had spoken. "You keep talking the way you just did and you're going to be the candidate," she repeated. It stayed in my mind. (Riess is now vice chairman of the district's campaign committee.)

Finally, I hit upon a new strategy. "All right, you're already committed," I began saying to people. "But if your man drops out, would you make me your second choice?" Almost without exception they agreed.

As the campaign wore on, I began to gain more confidence. Particularly in forums with the other candidates, I began to feel I was rising above the fray. At one particular GOP breakfast, I found people responding to me. I could see in their faces they regretted committing themselves to other candidates.

Still, the party leaders had their own ideas. In late March, Foley asked me to meet him at the Sheraton Hotel in Waterbury.

"I think your campaign is going nowhere," he said after we had swapped pleasantries. "You ought to think about pulling out and supporting somebody else."

I told him I was feeling more confident every day.

He went over the numbers. I had only about twenty-five delegates out of sixty-two needed to win. Everyone else was up around forty, except McLaughlin, who was bogging down. "There's talk about eliminating the low man after the first ballots," he said. "That's going to be you."

I protested that I wasn't ready to quit. He told me I'd better think about it.

A few days later I met with Steve Watson, one of my rivals. He had never held elected office and was considered to be something of a babe in arms. You have to be twenty-five to run for Congress and Perry Piscotti swore Watson was only twenty-three. His favorite expressions were "Gee whiz!" and "Golly!" His support was centered entirely in Danbury, the second-largest city in the district, where he was the favorite son. Most of the party veterans thought Moffett would humiliate him. He was the only candidate who made me feel like an old-timer.

Steve congratulated me on running a good campaign but said he didn't think I could win. "The numbers just aren't coming together for you, Gary," he said sympathetically. "Do you think you could give me your support? With Waterbury behind me, I know I could win it." Waterbury was by far the largest city in the district. The second- and third-largest towns' together would just equal Waterbury's delegate count.

"Steve, a lot of people could win if they had Waterbury." We left it at that.

The following week McLaughlin wanted to have lunch. "Gary, I think it's your votes that are keeping me from getting the nomination," he started. "I'm the only guy that can beat Moffett. He's liberal on everything but I'm liberal on social issues and conservative on fiscal issues. People like that. My supporters have talked to Santopietro, and he said if you were out of the race there's a good chance they would support me. With Waterbury I could win it all."

I knew this wasn't true, since the Santopietro people despised McLaughlin, calling him the "Woodbury preppie." Still, I didn't want to disappoint him.

"Jamie, a lot of people could win if they had Waterbury."

With my waistline rapidly expanding, I was relieved when Warren Sarasin called and said he *didn't* want to have lunch. He just wanted to talk. He had spoken with Perry Piscotti, who said the boys still supported me but might switch to him if the convention deadlocked. He asked if I would quit so the boys could come into his camp. "I know I can win it with Waterbury," he concluded.

"I know, Warren," I said. "I've heard that before."

Finally, Alan Schlesinger called. A onetime all-state football player and Wharton School of Business graduate, he had made one previous run for Congress. "People are impressed with the way you're making your case," he said. "You've definitely made a mark for your future. But it isn't going to happen now."

I asked if he had heard about the low-man-out rule.

"I have and I'm very sensitive about that," he said. "I'm Jewish and there aren't many Jewish voters in the district, just like there aren't many black people. Frankly, I'm hoping that you will support me and once you get out . . . if you are out . . . I mean . . . I don't know what's going to happen." By this time he was sputtering.

"I'm hoping you'll give your support to me," he prattled on. "I'm still negotiating with Joe and Perry but I'm not getting anywhere. Frankly, I think they're going to go for Sarasin, of all people. I certainly don't want him to get the nomination. I know I could win this thing if I just had Waterbury."

As I hung up, I realized I had the one thing that all the other candidates desired: the support of Waterbury. As I kept telling everybody, I was the only candidate who had carried the district, in my campaign for state comptroller in 1986. I was a popular alderman in the key city. Even though I had entered late, I had already raised one hundred fifty thousand dollars—more than any other candidate. Despite my low delegate count, there was a certain logic to my candidacy.

Still, I couldn't count on Waterbury forever. I remembered how my hometown support had evaporated during my run for state chairman in 1987. On the eve of the convention, Mayor Santopietro called me into his office. Piscotti, Vitarelli, and the Giacomi brothers were there.

"Give me a list of your supporters," Joe began.

One by one, I gave him the names. Just as rapidly, he began knocking each one down. That one wasn't in my camp. On and on it went.

Finally, Mayor Joe slammed down his fist. "You haven't done a single goddamn thing," he screamed. "You haven't gotten any support. All you've got is what we already gave you. Without Waterbury's delegates, you have one vote." With that he stormed out of the room.

"I have a number of people who are going to support me on the second or third ballots," I hollered after him.

"Look, we're in a jam here," Perry took up, hefting himself out of his chair. "We're supporting you, but we can't go on forever. We don't want to wake up and find that Steve Watson or Alan Schlesinger is the candidate. We want to be the kingmakers. We don't want to go down with you. If you can't make it, we want to decide who does."

"I can get the nomination given enough time," I explained patiently. "If we make it through four or five ballots, I can make my big move . . . a lot of people have said they'll switch to me."

"We may never get to a fourth ballot," exploded Vitarelli. "That's what we're worried about."

The phone rang and Piscotti stepped away. As we argued, Perry started shouting into the phone. "We didn't say the third ballot!"

He listened a moment, then turned to the room. "What about the fourth ballot?" he asked no one in particular.

"What's this about the fourth ballot?" I asked everyone.

"We have to let Sarasin's people know when we're going to switch to him," Perry said abstractly.

"Unacceptable!" I shouted, jumping out of my chair. "That's not what we agreed to." My fate was being decided right in front of my eyes.

"Let me get back to you," Perry shouted into the phone and hung up.

Just then Mayor Santopietro came back into the room. "You guys got this ironed out yet?" he asked cheerfully.

Perry shrugged.

"I'm going to do what I have to do," I admonished. "If necessary, I will file a lawsuit against the party for handicapping my chances by imposing the low-man rule."

Everyone knew it was an empty threat. If I filed suit, the courts would most likely dismiss the case.

The Connecticut Republican Convention was held on a steamy night in July at the Oxford Tavern. The mood was festive but apprehensive. All the candidates had tents or vans where they entertained their delegates as well as the general public. I made the mistake of having an open bar. My tent was well populated. The other candidates, I learned later, had cash bars. All that free booze still didn't wash away the impression that I was on a mission impossible.

Soon four hundred sweltering bodies were packed into the

overheated convention room. People hung from the rafters. There was no air-conditioning. The only relief—as far as I was concerned—was the news that the low-man rule had been eliminated, at least for the first few rounds.

On the first ballot, I received twenty-one votes. I was the dreaded low man. On the second, everything stayed the same.

Then votes started to shift. On the third ballot, a couple of Jamie McLaughlin's delegates came over to me. I moved into fourth place. On the fourth ballot, Jamie slipped again. He fell to fourteen while I rose to twenty-eight.

After every ballot, each candidate huddled with his troops and advisers. Then we worked the room, urging people who were leaning our way to take the plunge.

After the fourth ballot, I ran into McLaughlin outside the hall. "Those Waterbury bastards are a bunch of liars," he exploded. "They said they were going to come over to me and they didn't." I knew he was the only one who had believed this. He went off to have a few words with Dick Bozzuto, a former gubernatorial candidate and one of his key supporters, then came storming back. "I'm through," he announced. "I'm throwing in the towel."

"Jamie, before you make your announcement, can I rely on the support of your delegates? You said you'd support me if you dropped out of the race."

He looked stunned. "I don't know what my delegates are going to do," he sputtered. "I can't dictate anything."

Then the Woodbury preppie reentered the convention room to announce the withdrawal of his candidacy. He got a friendly ovation. I realized I was back in last place.

As we waited for the fifth ballot, I watched the Santopietro team careening around the floor, Perry Piscotti leading the charge, Bobby and Jack Giacomi, Paul Vitarelli, and Mayor Joe all tagging along behind. They seemed to be negotiating with Schlesinger's delegates. Then Sarasin's operatives cornered them. His team was well organized, with walkie-talkies and earpieces, incongruously efficient amidst the general pandemonium.

Just as the balloting was about to start, the dreaded announcement came. The fifth ballot would be low man out. Apparently Sarasin's people had persuaded the chair, but the move was also supported by the Santopietro people, who decided it was time to take on the kingmaker's role. As the voting began, a couple of delegates switched over to me. Then toward the end, chairman Dick Belden asked if any other delegates wanted to change their vote. A few more of Schlesinger's people moved my way. When the gavel finally came down and the vote was tallied, everyone was stunned. I was the third man by one vote. Sarasin had been eliminated!

Perry Piscotti detonated like a land mine. He threw his fists at the ceiling, screaming over the crowd. Shoving people out of the way, he beat a path to Sarasin's trailer.

"You goddamn idiots!" he screamed, unloading like a cement mixer. "You get us to adopt the low-man rule and then you end up biting the bullet yourself! What the hell kind of operation are you running here? Don't you guys know anything?"

I just stood there thinking, "These are my supporters?"

Apparently what happened was that Schlesinger had thrown a few delegates my way. Wanting to steal Waterbury from Sarasin and thinking the boys would never go for Steve Watson, he had a few of his supporters switch to me in order to knock Sarasin off the totem pole. Schlesinger's troops were ecstatic. They danced on the floor, high-fiving each other. Everyone else remained stunned at this O. Henry ending.

Yet I suspected immediately that my moment had arrived. I made it abundantly clear to Sarasin's vanquished soldiers that now was the time to support me—especially if they didn't want to see Schlesinger, who had outmaneuvered them, walk off with the prize.

As the balloting for the next round began, Schlesinger's people were still celebrating. The candidate himself strode around the room with a huge smile on his face. Only as the vote reached the midpoint did he realize what was happening. He was now the low man! When the votes were counted, young Steve Watson and I were the only candidates left in the race.

Schlesinger couldn't believe it. He looked as if he had swallowed a cigar. Meanwhile, my people were hugging and congratulating each other. Then good old Don Schmidt, my first town chairman, came rushing up. "It ain't over yet, Gary," he shouted. I knew he was right. We went right back to work.

Still, it was the best of all possible worlds. Watson was generally regarded as too wet behind the ears to run for Congress.
Moffett would eat him for breakfast. Still, running a black candidate in a 90 percent white district! Most people had to pinch
themselves.

As the final tally rang up, it became obvious that the delegates
had chosen uncertainty over naïveté. Most of Schlesinger's people
came over and I won handily. Out of four hundred people who
had entered the convention that night, I was probably the only
one who thought I had a real chance to win. Yet seven hours
later, there I was, the Republican Party's choice for the Fifth Congressional District.

"God did this for us," my sister Ruthie shouted over the
mayhem. "It's a miracle. He won't let you lose in November after
what He's done tonight."

There was only one way to find out if she was right.

EIGHT

The Race for Congress

ON A WARM morning in August 1990, I stood outside the Peter Paul Cadbury candy factory in Naugatuck, where I had been working only a few years before. As employees streamed through the factory gate, I greeted each one, trying to make eye contact. "Hi, I'm Gary Franks. I'm a Republican running for Congress."

As the crowd thinned out a bit, one heavyset woman with a huge handbag and a new permanent brushed by me without even a glance. "Hi, I'm Gary Franks, Republican running for Congress." She took another ten steps, then stopped in her tracks. Slowly she turned and walked back, sizing me up like a prize bull. "You're a Republican?" she said skeptically.

I nodded.

"Well, I'll think about it," she said and walked away.

"Does that happen often?" asked Nick Ravo, a reporter for the *New York Times*, who happened to be with me that morning.

"Once every few minutes," I told him. "When people see me campaigning, they automatically assume I'm a liberal Democrat. When I tell them I'm a Republican, they give me this strange look. 'You're a Republican?' they say. 'Well, I might give it some thought.'"

The race for the Fifth Congressional District in Connecticut was well under way. My opponent, Toby Moffett, had a tremendous advantage. He was about as close to being a nationally known figure as a congressman can be.

A veteran of Ralph Nader's early campaigns, Moffett was elected to Congress in 1974 from the sixth district (the northwestern part of the state) when he was barely thirty years old. A "Watergate Baby," Moffett went on to play a prominent role in the energy debates of that decade. Along with Congressmen Richard Ottinger of Westchester County, New York, and Andrew Maguire of Bergen County, New Jersey, he became the principal advocate for continuing price controls on oil—the disastrous policy that led to a decade-long "oil shortage." When President Reagan removed the price controls in his first month in office in 1981, the "oil shortages" disappeared and have never been heard of since.

In 1982, tiring of his work in Congress, Moffett abandoned his district and moved to Branford, on the Long Island Sound. From that vantage he challenged Republican Lowell Weicker for his U.S. Senate seat, losing by four percentage points (less than forty thousand votes). Having given up his seat in Congress, Moffett became what the *New York Times* called "a sort of Flying Dutchman of Connecticut politics, seen and heard everywhere, but apparently without a port to call home."

In 1986, he ran against incumbent Democratic Governor William O'Neill in a primary that badly splintered the Democratic Party. Both factions ended up bringing voter fraud charges in Waterbury. The incident left a bad taste that few people had gotten over.

After that defeat, Moffett renounced politics and became a TV anchorman in New Britain, seen and heard in every living room of the state. Still, the urge for elective office remained strong. Since all of Connecticut's congressional seats were held by long-term incumbents—three Republicans and three Democrats—there were few opportunities. But in 1989, when John Rowland indicated he would step down to run for governor, Moffett took a one-year lease on a house in Newtown while keeping his home in Branford. Despite this obvious ploy, he quickly emerged as the front-runner for Rowland's open seat.

Thus, Moffett had his strengths and weaknesses. He had name recognition and a record that would sit well with any liberal constituency. But his lust for public office had left him in a carpetbagger's role. We adopted Dion's hit tune "The Wanderer" as one of our theme songs. After people heard "Oh, I'm the type of guy/who likes to run around/I'm never in one place/I roam from town to town" a few times, they got the idea.

Moffett's other weakness was less visible but far more strategic. His extremely liberal politics didn't play well with the fifth district's blue-collar factory workers. These "Reagan Democrats" had moved solidly into the Republican column in 1984, but appeared to be drifting back by the end of the decade. Our objective was to keep them in the fold. More than one newspaper called the contest a "clear referendum on Reaganism."

When I called my first press conference a few days after winning the nomination, only the *Waterbury Republican*, the *Naugatuck Daily News*, and WATR Radio showed up. I walked them through my campaign themes and challenged Moffett to a series of debates. No one seemed very excited.

As we walked out, I heard one reporter ask, "Where's Moffett today?"

"He's on vacation," the other said, laughing. "He decided to take a couple of weeks off before starting his campaign."

I filed it away in my head: Moffett was overconfident.

At the state convention a week later, John Rowland won the gubernatorial nomination. As I roamed the floor, I was approached by Gerry Labriola Jr. His father, Gerry Sr., had played basketball at Yale and had scouted me at Sacred Heart. He was now a Naugatuck pediatrician and had served as state senator as well as making unsuccessful runs for governor and lieutenant governor.

"Gary, I can't tell you how proud we are that you got the nomination," he greeted me.

"I appreciate it, Gerry."

"Listen, Gary, my father would like to be your campaign manager."

"I appreciate it, Gerry, but I don't have enough money yet to pay anybody a decent salary."

"Don't worry. We'll do it for free. Dad is trying to establish a political consulting business with my older brother David and me. We need the experience."

At our first meeting, which was held at the Naugy Nook in Naugatuck, Gerry Sr. suggested we go negative against Moffett right off the bat. He proposed a series of unrelenting radio attacks. I was reluctant to start with that kind of approach, feeling I could get my message across without any mudslinging. So we settled on a strategy of getting my name before the public. One of our best devices turned out to be the "Gary Franks for Congress RV" van, which started rolling early in the campaign. I wasn't always aboard, but the van became a symbol of my unrelenting efforts and my deep roots in the district. I knew we were getting somewhere toward the end of the campaign when I heard Moffett remark: "I'm so tired of hearing about Gary Franks and that damned van."

Moffett, on the other hand, ran a celebrity-style campaign that only emphasized his tenuous ties to the district. At one point he brought in Robert Redford, who owns a vacation home in the southern part of the state. More important, it became clear that Moffett was more comfortable with affluent suburbanites than with the blue-collar factory towns that are the backbone of the fifth. Like many Democrats, he simply assumed that, as a legacy of the Roosevelt era, unionized factory workers were on his side. I knew differently.

On August 9, an account of my early-morning efforts at Peter Paul Cadbury appeared on the front page of the "Metro" section of the *New York Times*. "Mr. Franks expects to do well in Waterbury, which has about 15 percent of the district's registered voters and more than a third of its Democrats," wrote Ravo. "He also believes his Republican voter base in the rest of the district is strong because of its intense antipathy toward Mr. Moffett [and his liberal voting record]. Moreover, Mr. Rowland's coattails are likely to help Mr. Franks."

The next day, I got a call from Thelma Duggin, director of minority outreach at the Republican National Committee in Washington. I had turned up on their radar screen. Tony Welters, a prominent black Republican contributor from Virginia, did a fundraiser at his home and raised fifteen thousand dollars for my campaign. John Fund of the *Wall Street Journal* also did a story. That led to a call from Secretary of Housing and Urban Development Jack Kemp, who volunteered to do a fund-raiser in my district. It was my first one with a national figure. When Kemp arrived and I shook his hand, my first thought was, "He's awfully small to be a quarterback." But Kemp showed his famous tenacity before the crowd and helped raise seventeen thousand dollars—my first big contribution.

In September, Charlie Black, who had replaced the ailing Lee Atwater as acting chairman of the RNC, invited the top three black congressional candidates—Ken Blackwell, Al Brown, and me—to a press conference in Washington. Blackwell turned out to be a seasoned pro and stole the show. I was extremely nervous and probably didn't make a very good first impression.

That evening, however, I got a second chance. We addressed two hundred prominent black businesspeople at a function sponsored by the National Republican Congressional Committee. Ed Rollins, cochairman of the NRCC, presided. When my turn came to speak, Rollins stood at the side of the stage with drink in hand, nodding at almost everything I said. I gave an enthusiastic account of all the reasons I believed I could win my district. The crowd was very responsive. I believe it was that night they decided to give serious support to my campaign. Within a few weeks, *Jet* magazine also wrote a positive story. We felt things were beginning to take off.

By mid-September, Moffett realized he was in a race. What particularly aggravated him was my seeming ability to be everywhere at once. Night after night, I would show up at an event he had just addressed, or even be there when he arrived. It was obvious he would have to engage me in debates. Moffett complained that money was falling out of the sky into my campaign coffers, which was not quite true—but the NRCC helped considerably. High-profile administration officials appeared on my behalf. Secretary of Labor Elizabeth Dole, Secretary of Energy Admiral James D. Watkins, Secretary of Health and Human Services Louis Sullivan, and Bill Bennett, the Bush administration's drug czar, all visited the district, giving me publicity and helping me raise more money.

Moffett was a seasoned campaigner, make no mistake. In Congress he had been one of the youngest subcommittee chairmen on record and a tireless worker. His miscalculation was in thinking of himself as the incumbent—even though his seat had been in another district. Thus, when it came to debates, like any incumbent, Moffett wanted to limit the number, while in classic challenger style I was ready for as many forums as possible. Yet our polls showed me running in a dead heat where people knew who I was. If I became familiar enough to voters, substance might dominate.

Then the dirty tricks started. At several nearly all-white functions in the Naugatuck Valley, I suddenly found myself surrounded by a small gaggle of black boys. They were much more bedraggled than any children I had ever seen in Waterbury, yet they swarmed around and greeted me as if I were a long-lost father. The same group of boys showed up at two events. We were suspicious and passed word over to the Moffett campaign that there had better not be any more of this. The boys never showed up again.

Our first debate took place at Wilton High School. When we entered, Moffett was shocked to discover that one-third of the audience was black and almost two-thirds were solidly in my favor. The crowd applauded enthusiastically at everything I said and booed and hissed when Toby tried to score points. Even the moderator couldn't quiet them down. It was a frustrating evening for a front-runner. I kept my answers crisp and short while he had a tendency to ramble beyond the time limit. To me, it was a sure sign that he was starting to unravel. I felt confident I could match him in a debate forum.

At the end of our first debate, Moffett suddenly launched what turned out to be his big negative offensive against me. He called me a slumlord. He charged that I was a millionaire and that my buildings were full of housing violations. "How can he expect to run a congressional office serving half a million people when he can't even run his own business?" he asked. When the press rushed up to me after the debate, I told them it didn't surprise me that Moffett would leave no stone unthrown. I had just learned that he had written the other Democratic congressional candidates asking them to support him as president of the incoming freshman class.

The *Danbury New Times* did a story on my properties but most of the other papers ignored it. Then a week later, Moffett came out with a television commercial driving home the point.

The ad walked the hallway of my father's original three-decker, where I had lived as a child. Moffett pointed to some debris on the stairs and in the parking lot and said this was proof I abused my tenants and exploited them as a millionaire slumlord.

The facts were quite different. My real estate business had grown considerably and I owned more than a dozen properties around town. The original three-decker was in a family trust. Although we had never had any previous complaints, one group that had moved in only a month before began calling the health department and making loud complaints about missing light bulbs and damaged smoke alarms. We already had our suspicions that this group was a plant and were not surprised when they disappeared immediately after the election. One TV station, after reviewing all the facts, concluded: "One thing is for certain, Gary Franks is not a slumlord."

To my mind, Moffett was hitting below the belt, taking aim at my origins while posing as a socially concerned liberal. Granted, my childhood home might not look beautiful on television, but it was a typical-looking three-family home. It didn't seem as if that should be held against me.

We could see the uglier side of this campaign in the many FRANKS FOR CONGRESS lawn signs that ended up with "nigger" scrawled across them, or the late-night phone calls in which our supporters were asked, "You're not really going to vote for that nigger, are you?"

Rather than see my campaign undermined by this blatant racism, I decided to go public. In the middle of the next debate, on live television, I proclaimed: "I'm not going to blame you, Toby Moffett, because some of the people within your organization are allegedly calling voters in the middle of the night and asking them, 'You're not really going to vote for that nigger, are you?' I'm not going to blame you because I can drive down the streets of Ansonia, Waterbury, and other parts of this district and see 'nigger' scrawled on my yard signs."

Moffett sat in shock. He finally stammered that if such a thing were happening in his organization, it would cease immediately. He added that he did not condone any of that type of activity nor did he believe anyone in his campaign would do such a thing. But we had strong feelings that his campaign was behind it. After that, there were very few unseemly incidents.

For our part, we did get into trouble for going over the line a bit as well. At one point, my staff ran a TV ad showing people dancing in bell-bottomed trousers and other wild scenes from the 1970s, all presided over by President Jimmy Carter. A picture of Moffett from that era showed him wearing much longer hair. "Toby Moffett is a man from the past who supported Jimmy Carter's policies of runaway inflation," said a voiceover. I had discussed producing such a spot with Russ Schriefer and Stuart Stevens, my campaign advisers, but had not authorized it for airplay. When I heard it was being run, I stopped it immediately. I wanted to keep the tone of the campaign as elevated as possible. Ironically, after running only one day, this spot won Stevens a national award as one of the best political ads of the 1990 campaign.

In late October, we got our biggest boost when President George Bush and his wife, Barbara, came to campaign in my district. Mrs. Bush arrived first and helped raise twenty-five thousand dollars. The president was delayed because of his involvement in the infamous 1990 budget deal, but finally made it for a fund-raiser at the Waterbury Sheraton. The select crowd of 140 guests brought me another seventy thousand dollars.

After the event, President Bush, John Rowland, and I jumped into the limousine for a drive to Stamford, where the commander in chief was to appear at another fund-raiser in support of John's gubernatorial campaign. As we left the parking lot, we were met by a crowd of black demonstrators protesting the president's recent veto of the 1990 civil rights bill. "Shame on Franks!" "Shame on Bush!" they chanted as our limo roared past.

The three of us sat in glum silence. I could almost read the president's mind. "What am I doing here supporting this black candidate when he can't even win black support in his own district?" he was saying to himself.

I had done so well in previous debates with Moffett that I was particularly looking forward to the last one, only five days before the election. However, it was not to be. A few hours before I was to take the stage, while we were campaigning in Danbury, Donna started complaining of a pain in her stomach. It became so bad that she could barely sit up. Then we found she was bleeding. I rushed her to Danbury Hospital. I hoped to get back to Waterbury in time for the debate, but as Donna's pain grew worse, it became obvious that I wasn't going to make it. I called back and apologized to the sponsors but said my wife appeared to be in immediate danger. "One thing we can tell you," the nurses and doctor kept reassuring me. "Your wife's not pregnant."

Four hours later, the beaming staff doctor emerged once again. "I have good news and I have bad news. Which would you like to hear first?"

"Give me the bad news first."

"You're going to lose your number one campaigner for the rest of the election."

"What's the good news?"

"You're going to be a daddy. We were wrong. Your wife is pregnant. The fetus is wedged in the fallopian tube. With proper rest, however, it should settle down into the womb and you won't lose it."

When I got back to campaign headquarters, every TV station was waiting. I appeared live on several eleven o'clock news shows to tell everyone that Donna was pregnant. Missing the debate became a huge boost for my campaign. My numbers took a particularly big jump among women aged nineteen to forty-five, who had always been my biggest skeptics. They appreciated the idea that I was willing to put my wife's well-being above political issues. I have generally had strong support among women voters ever since.

Although we were making headway, the numbers still looked bad. A weekend before the election, Neil Newhouse, my campaign pollster, called to say we were still trailing by a significant margin—eight percentage points with a four-point margin of error. I was doing well with Italians and the staunch Republicans in the suburban parts of my districts, but the city vote wasn't swinging my way.

"How am I doing among blacks and Hispanics?" I asked.

"Well, we really can't give you a number," he said.

"What do you mean you can't give me a number?"

After a long pause, Neil replied, "We're assuming you're going to lose that vote."

"How can you assume that?"

"The sampling in your district is just too small—nine percent of the vote. We're applying Ken Blackwell's numbers in Cincinnati to your district. He's doing badly. We're assuming you won't do any better."

"But that's not a realistic assumption. I think I can do very well here."

"You may be right, Gary, but we don't have anything to verify it."

B. J. Cooper, a Waterbury native and communications director of the RNC, who was volunteering in my campaign, came on the phone. "Look, Gary, we appreciate your effort," he said. "You're having a big impact. All we're saying is that you'd better have two speeches ready—a victory and a concession—just in case."

On election night my supporters assembled at the Elton Hotel in Waterbury. The place had a special significance for me. As a seven-year-old, thirty years earlier, I had sat on a fireman's shoulders one cold November night and watched John F. Kennedy speak from the balcony in one of his last appearances of his 1960 presidential campaign. It was my first experience of politics—one that I have never forgotten.

Standing outside one polling site at 5:00 P.M., we got a piece of good news. The Waterbury absentee ballots were announced and we had broken even. Moffett, who was there, was distraught. Democrats outnumber Republicans three to one in Waterbury. I had done very little on absentees, but John Rowland had run an excellent absentee ballot campaign. I benefited from his efforts. It was a good omen.

As the polls closed at 8:00 P.M., the predominantly Democratic towns announced their results very quickly. This created the impression that Moffett was running away with the race. By 9:00 P.M., Dan Rather had told national audiences that Moffett was the projected winner in Connecticut's fifth district. He had to glance down at his notes to remember my name.

Still, we weren't discouraged. We had exceeded our expectations in Ansonia, Meriden, and the borough of Naugatuck. When Waterbury announced that Moffett and I had split the vote down the middle, we knew we had it made. As the late returns began to trickle in from the suburban portions of the district, things turned our way.

Sure enough, I ended up winning seventeen of the twenty-five towns and cities in the district. Around 10:00 P.M., it was announced I was nearly ten thousand votes and five percentage points ahead. A few minutes later, Toby Moffett marched downstairs to address his supporters at the Holiday Inn in Waterbury. Not having heard about the dramatic changes, they thought he was declaring victory. Instead, a deeply subdued candidate announced the race was over. "This is not a victory party," he told them. "I've lost."

At the Elton, where our people were celebrating wildly, Larry Cirignallo rushed up to me and Donna and shouted that the president was on the phone.

"How are you doing?" I heard George Bush's voice at the other end of the line.

"Very well, Mr. President. We won."

"I've gotten conflicting reports on your election. Has Moffett conceded?"

"Yes, Mr. President. It's over."

"Well, congratulations, Gary. I look forward to working with you down here in Washington."

Donna hugged me, and somebody snapped a picture. It appeared in *Time* magazine.

That night was the culmination of a dream everyone once thought impossible—that a black man could win an election by running on the issues in a predominantly white congressional district. Ours may not yet be a truly color-blind society, but there is no question we are steadily moving in the right direction.

As for my own reaction, all I could say, then and now, is, "God bless America."

Welcome to the House of Representatives

T HE DAY AFTER the election, I was asked to appear on *Nightline* as part of a group of newly elected officials. The panel consisted of Bernie Sanders, representative from Vermont and Congress's only Socialist; ultraliberal Paul David Wellstone, senator from Minnesota; Christine Todd Whitman, who had given Sen. Bill Bradley the scare of his life in New Jersey; and me, the anomalous black conservative Republican. Right away, I was being grouped with the "political oddballs." I also graced the cover of *USA Today*'s Sunday magazine as one of the most promising leaders for the 1990s.

By late November, I was busy preparing myself for the transition from a part-time alderman representing 110,000 people to a full-time congressman representing 500,000 people. For my district office, I picked the Federal Post Office Building in downtown Waterbury, near the Elton Hotel. The Grand Dragon of the Ku Klux Klan, who lived in Shelton, moved shortly after my election. (Even to this day, the Klan still rallies regularly in Meriden, which is in my district.)

Watching C-Span one afternoon, I found myself witnessing a press conference with Amelia Parker, executive director of the Congressional Black Caucus, before a group of mostly black journalists. Suddenly, from off-camera, one of the reporters mentioned my name. "What will the CBC be like now that a Republican like Gary Franks is a member?" he asked.

"We've had several Republican members before, representing areas from the Caribbean," Parker responded.

"Yes, but they weren't voting members."

"The Congressional Black Caucus is a nonpartisan organization," she affirmed. "We will have no trouble accommodating Mr. Franks. He will be welcomed just like any other black member of Congress."

I was extremely encouraged by her remarks. Contrary to everyone's expectations, Ken Blackwell and Al Brown had both lost their races. When the 102d Congress convened in January, I would be the only black Republican member.

In fact, everyone I had met was asking me if I would join the Black Caucus. Jack Kemp had made it a first order of business when he campaigned for me in September. The CBC had a reputation for taking extremely liberal positions on every issue. At that very moment, they were opposing any United States military actions in Kuwait on the grounds that a disproportionate share of American blacks would be fighting in combat.

"Aren't you hesitant about joining such a bunch of liberals?" people would ask.

"Not at all," I would reply. "They're just a group of African Americans who happen to be members of Congress. Now they will have an African American Republican member of Congress."

The January swearing-in ceremony was like a dream come true. I walked into the Capitol, where Henry Clay, Abraham Lincoln, and John F. Kennedy had once served, and felt almost overcome with emotion. I vowed that I would uphold my oath of office and serve my constituents as honestly and diligently as any man or woman who had ever served before me.

As I entered the main door with my daughter Azia, I asked the doorman where I should sit. "Sit anywhere," he said politely.

"No, you don't understand," I said. "I'm Gary Franks, from Connecticut. I'm a newly elected member. Where's my seat?"

"You can sit anywhere," he repeated. "What party are you?"

"I'm a Republican."

"Well, Democrats usually sit over here," he said, pointing to the left side of the chamber. "Republicans sit there. But you can sit anywhere you like."

I had never realized it, but other than for the leadership, there are no assigned seats in the House of Representatives. I took a seat on the right, three rows from the leadership desk.

Right after the swearing-in, Bob Michel, the minority leader, took three quick steps up the aisle and shook my hand. "Welcome to the House of Representatives," he said. His two sons had played basketball with me at Yale and he often attended our games. Still, I was immensely touched by his gesture.

The Congressional Black Caucus's reception in the Cannon House Building a few hours later was something altogether different. Several new black members had been elected and there was an air of festivity. Bill Cosby and R&B singer Barry White were there, and Thurgood Marshall—only a few months before his retirement—was the special guest. He administered the ceremonial oath of office to the CBC members.

If my constituents were excited about their new representative, the press seemed insatiable. TV cameras literally followed me nonstop for the first few days. I couldn't go from one point on the Hill to another without a string of reporters tailing me.

One of the best moments of the first month was an appearance before the National Press Club. It was pretty much the same cast of "oddballs" that had appeared on *Nightline*—me, Bernie Sanders, and David Wellstone, plus Eleanor Holmes Norton, the nonvoting congressional representative from the District of Columbia. Sen. Al Gore, Jack Kemp, and Congressman Ron Dellums of California were in the audience.

We were asked to keep our remarks light, but few of the other speakers managed to do so. Norton was mildly funny but Wellstone couldn't tell a joke to save his neck and Sanders didn't seem to have any sense of humor.

When my turn came, I told the audience about the problems I had trying to convince one black woman to vote for me during my first run for Waterbury alderman.

" 'Let's talk issues,' I had said to her. 'We're being overtaxed in this city. Our property tax is one of the highest in the region. People are leaving Waterbury and companies won't move in, costing the city jobs. I want to do something about it.'

"The woman nodded her head in agreement the whole time I spoke, but when I finished she shook her head and said, 'Yes, but you're a Republican.'

"'We have one of Connecticut's highest crime rates. For a town our size, we rank in the highest percentile for serious crime. We need more police officers on the street. We need to improve the technology in the police department. I will fight for that.'

"'Yes, but you're a Republican,' she said.

"'The present Democratic administration has been in power for ten years. The Justice Department has looked at their activities and found them questionable or worse. We need a city government that is beyond reproach and earns the respect of the people it serves. Can I have your vote?'

"'But you're a Republican.'

"Finally, I got exasperated. I looked the lady dead in her eyes and said, 'Mother, I am your son and I need your vote.'"

The audience cracked up. I left that meeting feeling I might have a future in Washington after all; if not as a politican, maybe as a comedian. (Actually, my mother has always been a Republican. It was really my aunt, a lifelong Democrat, with whom this conversation took place.)

By the end of the first three months of 1991, I had visited the White House at least five times. In some cases, the entire freshman class was invited. At other times, the president invited specific members of Congress to build support for his policies, particularly during the debate on the Persian Gulf War. It seemed as if George Bush liked having me around.

On our first visit, the president pulled me aside and wanted to know how things were going.

"Well, I'm getting adjusted," I said.

He told me he thought I would do a fine job. Then he looked me in the eye. "Gary, on this civil rights bill that's coming up . . ." He leaned over and put his arm around my shoulder. "Don't feel you have to support me on this issue. I've got all the people in this room to look after me." He gestured around him. "You're pretty much out there by yourself. If you feel you can't stick with me on this effort, I'll understand. The most important thing for me is that you come back for another term."

"Mr. President, I don't see any problem in supporting you on this," I said. "In fact, I'm looking forward to playing an active role. I've already asked to be on the House Republican task force on civil rights."

A smile settled on his face, but it was a smile that suggested disbelief. "Well, do what you think is right," he said. "If you have any problems, just contact me through Fred McClure."

The president knew that, by supporting his stand, I would have to oppose affirmative action quotas. That might open me up to criticism. Although increasingly resented by whites—including most of my constituents—quota-like programs had strong support among blacks and were gospel within the Black Caucus. The president understood my dilemma and I understood his. Even today, I appreciate his concern for my situation.

My work on the task force turned out to be complex indeed. I saw myself as a mediator between extreme liberals such as Sen. Edward Kennedy, who I felt wanted outright quotas in the bill, and extreme conservatives such as Congressman Henry Hyde of Illinois, who obviously had other things in mind.

The negotiations kept me shuttling up and down Pennsylvania Avenue and back and forth across the ideological spectrum. President Bush vetoed Congress's first effort, on the grounds that it contained quotas. When the Republican task force unveiled its second effort, I had my first chance to speak before a national press conference. In one memorable meeting, I sat with Representatives Maxine Waters from Los Angeles and Charles Rangel from New York, both stalwarts for quota-like programs, while Teddy Kennedy made a pitch for compromise language that President Bush had agreed to sign.

In the end, we forged a piece of legislation that reduced racial discrimination without instituting racial quotas. After plenty of work, the measure drew widespread support on Capitol Hill. It passed both houses by the highest margins of any civil rights bill in history. It was an effort of which I am still extremely proud.

*   *   *

On June 11, 1991, my daughter Jessica Lynn was born. Soon after, I decided to take her to Washington. My wife brought her, cradled in her arms, into the regular noontime meeting of the Congressional Black Caucus in the Capitol Building. I immediately ran into Charles Rangel of New York, one of the senior members. After cooing over Jessica for a few moments, Rangel asked when she was born. When I told him, he replied, "Franks, there may be hope for you after all. Your daughter was born on my birthday."

"I prefer to think she was born one day before George Bush's birthday." We both laughed.

As the meeting convened, however, I realized things were far more tense than usual. Congressman Craig Washington encouraged my wife to leave. This was a business meeting, he said, and the members did not want to mince words in front of spouses and newborns. Bill Jefferson, congressman from Louisiana, was kind enough to chat with my wife for a few moments before she made a quick departure.

The topic of the day, it emerged, was President Bush's nomination of Clarence Thomas to the U.S. Supreme Court. Almost before the meeting had been called to order, Craig Washington declared, "The caucus should come out immediately in opposition to this nomination."

I raised my hand and wondered out loud why we were making this move so hastily without even knowing much about Mr. Thomas.

Congressman John Conyers of Michigan said we all knew Thomas's qualifications from his appointment to the District of Columbia Court of Appeals.

"Well, you didn't contest that appointment," I responded.

"We did but we didn't fight hard enough," snapped Conyers.

"I'm not prepared to cast a vote on this until I learn more about Clarence Thomas," I said. "In fact, I'm kind of leaning toward supporting him."

"We're not surprised to hear that," Representative Washington smirked.

"According to this morning's issue of *USA Today*, the majority of black people are supportive of Thomas."

"That's because they don't know him!" shouted Washington. "They're just supporting him because he's a brother."

"But the polls are showing he's in sync with what most blacks are thinking."

"Look, we'd rather have no black on the Supreme Court and take our chances on the 1992 election than have someone like Clarence Thomas."

Chairman Ed Towns of New York ended the discussion abruptly. "We're going to entertain a motion on opposing Clarence Thomas's nomination to the Supreme Court," he announced.

The motion passed twenty-five to one; I was the lone dissenter.

I had walked into the meeting hoping to let my wife and little girl see what Daddy does for a living. I left feeling as if I had just stepped on a roller coaster. The ride wouldn't end soon.

The next day I remembered President Bush's standing offer that whenever I needed help I could contact his aide, Fred McClure. I decided to take him up on it. I called McClure and told him my dilemma. Was there any way I could meet Clarence Thomas to clarify things in my own mind?

"I don't think that's going to be possible," said McClure decidedly. "Nobody in the House is being given access—not even Newt Gingrich and they're both from Georgia."

"Well, I'm not exactly a typical House member," I said. "The press is already swarming all over me. If you want me to help you, I should be as well versed as possible."

McClure began to have second thoughts. "I see what you're saying," he said. "Let me get back to you in a bit."

Two hours later, McClure called. "Here's what will happen. Within the next twenty-four hours, you'll get a phone call from Senator John Danforth [the Missouri Republican who was shepherding the nomination through the Senate]. He will ask you over to his office. Don't be surprised if you're greeted by another individual while you're there."

Like clockwork, I soon received the call. As I toured the Russell Building for the first time, I realized how much better it is to be a senator than a congressman. Not only was Danforth's office far bigger than mine, it also had a fireplace. (I realize now that all senators have one.) As I walked into his inner sanctum, I got my first glimpse of Clarence Thomas. He was shorter and more barrel-chested than I had anticipated.

"So you're the guy who's been fighting for me on the House side," said Thomas, shaking hands. I was surprised to realize he knew me.

"I just wanted to find out a bit more about the guy I'm fighting for," I said.

"Well, you've got your work cut out. I know how difficult it's going to be over in that Black Caucus," he said.

"Yeah, those people aren't very fond of you." We laughed uproariously. Danforth managed a chuckle as well, although he seemed distinctly ill at ease.

Clarence and I reviewed some of the objections being made by the Black Caucus. I told him there were specific complaints about the way he had run the Equal Employment Opportunity Commission after taking over for Eleanor Holmes Norton.

"Look, when I took over, that place was a mess," he countered. "There was a huge backlog of cases all over the country. Eleanor still had people using typewriters. We brought in computers and moved the commission into the modern age. We cleaned up the backlog and finally got things moving again. Go ask the people who work there." I later took his advice and talked to a whole gang of people at EEOC. They backed him up completely.

Judge Thomas and I talked for about twenty minutes. He was very open and friendly. He expressed appreciation that my lone vote had kept the condemnation of the Black Caucus from being unanimous. "It's going to be a long tough battle," he concluded, "but I'm confident."

Within a few months, of course, Thomas's nomination had gone from being an ideological battle to a grueling national ordeal over the issue of sexual harassment. I thought of our meeting many times while Anita Hill's charges were being broadcast into every living room in the country. Seeing how cheerful and confident Thomas had been that morning, it was devastating to see him going through the agony of refuting the charges.

In the end, the Senate decided that Hill's accusations were too unsubstantiated to block the nomination of a highly qualified judge. It gave me particularly great pleasure to see President Bush and the GOP leadership stand beside Thomas throughout the controversy. When the battle was finally won, my wife and I were proud to be part of Justice Thomas's swearing-in ceremony on the White House lawn. The firm handshake that he gave me indicated that he had weathered an ordeal that few other men could have endured. He thanked me for my support. I am confident Justice Clarence Thomas will eventually be vindicated through his outstanding work on the Supreme Court.

As exciting as my first year in Congress had been, it was almost overshadowed by events back home. In 1990, the *Waterbury Republican* began a series of stories that uncovered a racket that Mayor Santopietro and the Republican administration had been perpetrating on the people of Waterbury for many years.

During early 1990, a couple of Connecticut banks began to fail. As regulators went over the books, they found a whole network of real estate holding companies of which Mayor Santopietro, Perry Piscotti, and most of the Republican administration were members. These companies had regularly bought poorly valued Waterbury properties, then brought them before the zoning commission for major zoning changes, usually to allow condominiums. The supermarket that the administration had wanted to convert to a grade school had also been owned by another Santopietro-related group.

Because the Republicans controlled all the boards, these changes generally went through—although often over protests from neighboring residents. It was only when I began to make objections that things started to unravel. That was the reason why I had been kicked off the zoning board and moved to the library board as quickly as possible.

During my first months in Congress, I gave long depositions to the prosecutor's office, telling of my experiences with the administration. They decided I would be one of their best witnesses. I told them I would be willing to help. They agreed not to call me unless it was absolutely necessary, but told me I should be ready.

As the trial opened in 1991, it became obvious that much was at stake—and strange things started to occur. Before the trial even began, the father of one of the prosecution witnesses was found dead in his basement, facedown in an inoperable, cast-iron bathtub full of water. The story was not widely reported. During the trial, the brother of Joe Tramuta, another star prosecution witness, was also found dead. Supposedly he had tripped, fallen headfirst into his own toilet, and then flushed it, drowning himself. Tramuta himself is now believed to be in a federal witness-protection program, living under an assumed name.

I began to remember that I had been shadowed by Waterbury police officers during my conflicts with the Santopietro administration over zoning matters. The officers had become so familiar that I waved to them. I assumed at the time that it had something to do with my responsibilities in city government, but now I began to wonder.

Then another witness had a strange experience. Joe Carrah had been in charge of the city's federal job training grants, which Mayor Santopietro had allegedly used for personal expenses. The morning Carrah left home to testify in court, he began to feel woozy. He pulled to the side of the road and avoided an accident, but had to be hospitalized. It was found he had been drugged. He eventually recovered and was able to testify before pleading guilty himself to misuse of government funds.

In the middle of the trial, Perry Piscotti had lunch with the relative of another witness near the courthouse and urged her to encourage the witness to be forgetful on the stand. "Just tell them she can't remember anything," he told her. Unfortunately for Perry, his waitress that day was an undercover police officer wired with a tape recorder. Piscotti had an obstruction-of-justice charge tacked onto his indictment.

In this sinister atmosphere, I felt a great deal of trepidation about being the high-profile witness. My family and I are Waterbury residents and like to mingle as much as possible. Nevertheless, in March I got the call from Assistant U.S. Attorney Holly Fitzsimmons. She wanted me to testify in three days.

Naturally, I had mixed feelings walking into the courtroom. These men had been my political mentors. They gave me my first break. I had never seen any trace of racial prejudice in them, and although I didn't always enjoy their company, I had gotten to like them. Yet they had violated a public trust in a way I found utterly inexcusable. Had I found out what was going on during my term as alderman, I would have turned them in immediately. There was no question in my mind that I had to testify.

The TV crews and reporters were out in force as I arrived at the courthouse. As I sat in the waiting room, I told Rick Genua, my chief of staff, "This is really going to be tough. I'm going to be facing the families of all those guys."

"Gary, just remember, it was their action that brought them here," Rick said. "If you hadn't been so honest, your family might be sitting out there, too."

"I hear what you're saying, Rick."

The witness before me had said that Gary Franks was one of the principal obstacles to the entire scheme because I had opposed so many zoning changes. The stage was set. As I took the stand, I looked directly over at the boys, thinking how many times we had met in better days to discuss the future of our city. Although the evidence seemed to be mounting against them, they still looked confident, perhaps a little cocky.

Assistant U.S. Attorney Fitzsimmons quizzed me on a series of votes that had come before the zoning board. She had prepared a series of charts showing how my votes had played an obstructionist role. She asked me about the reaction of other party members to my opposition and got me to recount my abrupt removal from the zoning board after one term.

"Congressman, when you were reassigned to the library board and the Civil Service Commission, were these voting positions?"

"No."

"What were your responsibilities?"

"I conveyed the board of aldermen's feelings about certain issues, but my main job was to ferry comments from the library board back to the board of aldermen."

Now I faced cross-examination by their attorney.

"Congressman, isn't it true that the Santopietro people, Joe Santopietro and Perry Piscotti, got you involved in politics, assisted you when you were selected to run for state comptroller in 1986, helped you with your speech, and were very vocal in your support at the state convention?"

"That's true."

"And isn't it true that they supported you at the convention that nominated you for your present seat in Congress?"

"They supported me for a few ballots, but they also supported 'low man out,' knowing I was the low man. They were prepared to throw their votes to Warren Sarasin until he was eliminated in a surprise intrigue involving Alan Schlesinger. If Sarasin had not been eliminated, I probably would have lost their support."

He saw that line of questioning wasn't working and swiftly changed directions.

"Mr. Franks, at any time did Alderman Giacomi or Alderman Vitarelli ask you to do anything beyond what you might be asked to do by minority whip Newt Gingrich?"

"Anytime they would pressure me to vote a certain way, they made their points clearly. They always kept it in a political context and never spoke of anything other than what would be good for the city of Waterbury."

"Thank you, no more questions."

A week later, the jury deliberated only a few hours before finding all the defendants guilty. Perry Piscotti received nine and a half years in jail and will be out in the year 2001. Mayor Santopietro was sentenced to nine years. Bobby Giacomi, Paul Vitarelli, and Fred Guisti, all city aldermen, got about three years apiece.

It was a horrifying betrayal of public trust. Yet miraculously it ended up improving relations between me and my constituents. They could see that I had acted honorably throughout and had always kept the public interest uppermost in my mind. This was important to me because I would need every bit of support I could get from them in my looming confrontation with the Congressional Black Caucus.

TEN

—◦◦◦—

The Black Caucus

R ACE RELATIONS affects each and every one of us. Even though my district is 90 percent white, I felt my constituents would be affected by what happens between black and white Americans. Being an African American myself, I also had a personal interest. For these reasons, I decided to join the Congressional Black Caucus.

The CBC meets at lunchtime every Wednesday. We have a meal and then conduct some business, usually relating to legislation or other public issues of the day. Congress is full of such caucuses—the women's caucus, the farm state caucus, the Irish caucus—but few of them meet as regularly or have as extensive a paid staff. Belonging to the Black Caucus was no small thing. My constituents paid five thousand dollars a year for the privilege.

Most of our Black Caucus meetings featured a rectangular seating arrangement. I usually made it a point not to sit near the head of the table but as close to the door as possible. This allowed swift and convenient exits in case the discussion got too tedious.

Early on, the members seemed to greet me with open arms. Sources told me all of them—except Bill Clay of Missouri—wanted me as a member. Clay made it clear he thought I would be an inappropriate addition because of my views toward African Americans. Nonetheless, nothing was ever said at the meetings about my acceptance as a member.

Ron Dellums of California was just stepping down as chairman, to be replaced by Edolphus Towns from Brooklyn. Everyone knew the dynamic Dellums would be a tough act to follow. With other offices opening up, I toyed with the idea of asking someone to put my name in nomination. Word got around and Bill Jefferson began joking about it. "Gary, do you want to be nominated for secretary or treasurer?" he asked aloud at one point. There were a few chuckles.

"I'll just take it one step at a time," I replied. "I'm just happy to be here as a member of Congress."

Some of the more senior members tried small talk. "You're from Connecticut," offered Charley Rangel, the veteran from Harlem, at one luncheon. "You must be a neighbor of mine."

I smiled. "You caused a big division in my family when you unseated Adam Clayton Powell Jr. in 1970," I told him.

"I was just a young upstart then," said Rangel.

"Adam's son is going to come along and knock off Charley one of these days," joked one veteran member.

"Bring the young man on," said Rangel with mock bravado. "Just bring him on."

The tense caucus room became a little cozier as we engaged in this banter.

"My college girlfriends were all big admirers of you gentlemen," I told them, trying to introduce a little conviviality.

"Well, you're not really a black congressman," said Rep. Harold Ford of Tennessee, souring the moment. "You're just a congressman who happens to be black and is representing white people."

"Let's not get into this right now," interrupted Chairman Towns. "Let's go around the room and hear what all the freshmen have to say about themselves. Let's start with you, Maxine."

Maxine Waters of Los Angeles began. She talked about her political career and how, unlike some others, she had endured "the black experience." Other freshmen followed with similar remarks. As it happened, my turn came last.

Amid a deafening hush, I began at last. "Some of you may be thinking that I have not shared 'the black experience.' I would disagree with you on that point. With the exception of John

Lewis [the Georgia congressman and veteran civil rights activist], I would wager that no one in this room has endured the racist experiences that I have been through in Connecticut.

"I am not from the Connecticut of George Bush, nor the Yale of George Bush. I was not born with a silver spoon in my mouth. My father was barely able to read or write. He had a sixth-grade education. My mother had a high school degree. Yet I am the only one of my parents' six children without an advanced college degree.

"My father worked in a brass mill for four decades. When we moved from one section of Waterbury to another, we were promptly greeted with a burning cross on our front yard from the Ku Klux Klan. We had threatening phone calls for several months. Even during my congressional campaign, I had 'nigger' scrawled on my yard signs. People were calling up my supporters saying, 'You're not going to vote for that nigger, are you?' "

I didn't think anyone had started breathing again, so I continued. "Unlike many of you, I do not come from parents who were second or third generation—educated. Unlike many of you, my entire lineage is African American as far as I know—not that that should mean anything.

"Yet, I do come from a district that is American, not just a district drawn up to represent only African Americans. When you look at the number of Italians and Irish and Poles and Hispanics and African Americans in my district, you realize it comes very close to the demographics of the entire country. I did not win the election by promoting the idea that I was black. In fact, if every black in my district had voted for me three or four times, I would still need significant support from whites as well in order to win."

"You beat Toby Moffett, didn't you?" Towns interrupted.

"That's right. I ran against a very powerful candidate."

"That Moffett is a tough son of a gun," said Representative Ford. "He was in my freshman class."

"You probably even gave money to his campaign," I countered. The Tennessee Democrat just shrugged and rolled his eyes toward the ridiculously high ceiling.

"In any case, I'm happy to be here and I hope you will be as attentive to my ideas for promoting the interests of African Americans as I intend to be to yours."

"Thank you very much, and we're happy to have you as a member," said Chairman Towns. "We are now a truly bipartisan organization."

"Besides, we may need you to work with George Bush," threw in Rep. Craig Washington.

He was right.

One of the first major issues on our agenda was the impending Persian Gulf War. Like most Democrats, the Black Caucus was adamantly opposed to any military action whatsoever. "Black boys are going to be disproportionately represented on the front lines," Maxine Waters told the meeting. "We're just sacrificing black lives for a conflict in which we have no interest." (This same argument was not used when the question arose of using force in Haiti years later. Most Black Caucus members supported military action.)

Everyone was extremely embarrassed a few weeks later, when the "Mother of All Battles" turned out to be a military shutout. To compound the embarrassment, this stunning success was directed by General Colin Powell, the nation's first black chairman of the Joint Chiefs of Staff. When General Powell came to address the caucus a few weeks later, only about half the members showed up.

One after another, Charley Rangel, Ed Towns, and Craig Washington all got up to throw themselves on Powell's mercy. They confessed they had opposed the war, but told how they had come to admire the Bush administration's decision to defend Kuwait and the masterful way in which Powell and his troops had performed.

When it came my turn, I couldn't resist. "General Powell," I began, "I'm proud to say I'm the only member in this room who supported you *before* the war was fought. The other members here didn't believe that you and the Bush administration would be able to handle this conflict in such an efficient manner, but I did. I'm happy to say I don't regret my faith in you and I'm proud that you were able to accomplish your objective in such an outstanding fashion."

The other members were more than a little vexed.

After the meeting, I stuck around to chat with the general. "I understand that when your parents left Jamaica, their first stop was in my district," I told him.

"That's true," Powell said. "My parents lived in Ansonia before they moved to the Bronx. We still have relatives there."

"That's close enough for me," I said. "As far as I'm concerned, you're a native of my district. I hope I can get you up there to speak sometime."

"I'll make it if I can," he said.

"By the way," I added, before he departed, "I just wanted to thank you for helping me get elected."

"How's that?" he asked. "I don't get involved in politics."

"Well, the mere fact of having an African American in Dwight Eisenhower's position has made it much easier for the people of my district to vote for me as one of 435 congressmen."

Powell posed with me for photographers while the other members maintained a respectful silence. He later recounted this same instance in his autobiography.

If there was one speaker notable for his absence in the Black Caucus during my first term, it was Douglas Wilder, governor of Virginia. As the highest-ranking black official in the country in a neighboring state, Wilder appeared to be a natural choice. Yet Wilder made the caucus members very uneasy. He was not a candidate who ran on racial grounds but who appealed to the general electorate. He was also a fiscal conservative who balanced Virginia's budget and turned Virginia into one of the two or three best-run states in the country. Wilder spent much of his time getting under the skin of New York's governor, Mario Cuomo, a great favorite of the caucus, who had been so profligate and irresponsible that his state had the lowest bond rating in the nation.

As the 1992 presidential campaign began, Wilder entered the race. What more exciting moment than the entry of a black governor as a serious contender for the presidency—another first for the nation. Yet the caucus completely avoided the issue. In fact, there was a quiet movement—much of it at the behest of Jesse Jackson—to talk down Wilder's presidential candidacy.

If there was one event to which we could have sold tickets

during my first term, however, it was the visit of Secretary of Housing and Urban Development Jack Kemp. The caucus's usual strategy was to intimidate whites and make them feel guilty. Most members of the administration didn't like that, so they stayed away. Kemp was the exception. He wasn't intimidated.

Although some of his aides seemed uncomfortable to be there, Kemp immediately launched into an animated pitch for Project HOPE—Housing Opportunities for People Everywhere. This is an attempt to interest public housing residents in buying their own apartments. By assuming ownership, Kemp argued, public housing tenants could build equity and participate more fully in American society. Buying these units would mean more than just pride of ownership and enhanced self-esteem. People could borrow against their houses to start small businesses—just as ordinary people often do. Or they could sell their unit and move out of public housing.

Kemp's presentation was longer than it should have been, perhaps because he used anecdotes to convey his points. Once he had finished talking, however, it was open season.

Bill Clay, because of his seniority, got first crack. "Mr. Secretary, the housing projects in my district are in such bad condition that they should either be renovated or destroyed. No sane person would want to own one of these units. There is no chance of them increasing in value and they will probably decrease. We are kidding ourselves to think any person would be gaining equity."

Maxine Waters judged the whole idea on whether anyone would want to buy a unit of public housing and place it right next to Jack Kemp's home. Charles Rangel was also critical, but very cordial to his former congressional colleague.

Then to everyone's surprise, some of the Southern representatives started expressing support for the idea. Louisiana's Bill Jefferson spoke in favor. Mississippi's Mike Espy—who later became Bill Clinton's secretary of agriculture before resigning under an ethical cloud—said he wanted to play a leading role if the idea ever became a reality. I also voiced my support.

"I don't want this to be a party-line issue," said Kemp, winding up. "The people in this room represent the conscience of this Congress. I want to get all the African American support I can."

I looked around the room in amazement. For the first time I had ever seen, the Black Caucus had actually divided on a major social issue. On every other subject, the vote had always been twenty-five to one, with me the lone dissenter. Now people were actually discussing an issue where there were logical choices involved.

When Project HOPE finally came before Congress, four Black Caucus members—Jefferson, Espy, Ford, and myself—all voted for it. The bill passed with bipartisan support. Secretary Kemp invited us up to his office for breakfast to celebrate the victory. I felt an extreme sense of satisfaction. It was perhaps the first time I felt we were making concrete progress on a major social issue.

In late April 1992, a jury in Simi Valley, California, acquitted five Los Angeles police officers of unnecessarily beating Rodney King after a high-speed traffic chase. All hell broke loose. By the time the smoke cleared, much of Los Angeles was a smoldering ruin. America had not seen a riot this bad in decades.

I was immediately summoned to the White House, along with Reverend Joseph Lowry of the Southern Christian Leadership Conference, Benjamin Hooks of the NAACP, John Jacobs of the Urban League, and many other black leaders. Sitting with President Bush were Vice President Dan Quayle, Secretary of State James Baker, and (for some reason) National Security Adviser Brent Scowcroft, who seemed to be nodding off. Of the black leaders, I was the only elected official in the room. (Maxine Waters, in whose district the riots had occurred, protested loudly and was admitted to the deliberations a few days later.)

Most of the civil rights leaders simply wanted to know what the president was going to do about the situation. As Joseph Lowry, the third speaker, repeated essentially the same things, I grew impatient. I interrupted and asked, "If the gentleman would yield . . . "

"I don't know what Mr. Franks is talking about, but he is not now in Congress. I am not about to yield to anyone. I am speaking and I don't want to be interrupted."

I smiled sheepishly and said, "Excuse me, I'll wait until you're finished." Everyone at the table was amused.

When my turn came, I stressed that it was important that the public perceive that justice had been done. Everyone I talked to—black and white—thought the verdict was unfair. I suggested that the president determine whether any federal civil rights laws had been broken and proceed with a federal prosecution, if possible. Everyone seemed to agree that was a good idea. Such a prosecution was eventually brought, and two of the officers were convicted.

What really upset me about the riots was that so much of the anger had been aimed at businesses owned by other ethnic groups, particularly Koreans. My background is small business, and I appreciate the tremendous effort that goes into running something as simple as a corner grocery store. Immigrant groups with tight-knit families are often successful at these businesses. For whatever reasons, blacks have not been as successful. This often creates resentments that are very unproductive to a community.

I reasoned that greater entrepreneurial effort would give blacks a greater stake in their own communities. Signs saying BLACK-OWNED BUSINESS, PLEASE DO NOT DESTROY were generally honored during the riots. If more blacks became business owners, Korean-owned businesses would not stand out so much, and maybe the resentment against commercial enterprises would abate. Dollars would circulate and recirculate within the neighborhood. The result? A more robust economy within these communities and greater community spirit.

While I was in college, I learned that General Foods had established the North Street Company, a subsidiary designed to help create more black entrepreneurs. Its goals were twofold: to provide capital and to offer the firm's administrative expertise.

Having studied Jack Kemp's efforts to establish "enterprise zones," I realized that only the bravest companies will locate their offices in marginal urban areas. Everything from traffic to contaminated waste sites is a problem, but the main deterrent is a legitimate fear of crime. Still, I believe, such firms are missing out on the largely untapped assets these areas have to offer: low property prices, a relatively low-cost workforce, and a consumer market hungering for greater choices. Many ambitious African and Hispanic Americans were ready and willing to revitalize these areas. The only things needed were money and know-how.

I introduced the Urban Entrepreneurs Opportunity Act in Congress. It was aimed at encouraging large corporations to participate in the rebirth of urban areas. Most of these companies were unwilling to launch new businesses in these locales. But if they could help budding entrepreneurs to do so, they might still enjoy tax and other benefits. The provisions of the bill were as follows:

+ Businesses would be able to deduct money lent to such ventures just as if they were contributions made to the United Way or other charities.
+ Businesses could be repaid these loans without losing the charitable tax deduction.
+ Businesses could use any jobs created through these ventures to meet government requirements for affirmative action or other regulations.

Businesses would be required to offer technical and administrative assistance in such areas as marketing, accounting, product development, and management in order to help ensure that these ventures would succeed. In order to avoid competition with local banks, such loans would have to be made at interest rates 1 to 2 percent above the rate for commercial bank loans.

Having worked for *Fortune* 500 companies, I was confident I could get some cooperation. If every company contributed just one million dollars each, we would build a half-billion-dollar pool that could inspire a renaissance in many of America's embattled communities. The bill would have allowed companies to contribute up to ten million dollars. Best of all, the federal government would not have to contribute one penny beyond the charitable tax exemptions granted for the contributions.

I began calling companies in my district to see if they were interested. John Rich, president of Hughes Optical Corporation in Danbury, expressed great enthusiasm. (Hughes has several large plants in Los Angeles.) The presidents of Aetna Insurance and

Pitney Bowes also expressed interest. Several other executives said they don't even approve of transactions of less than a million. It was small potatoes for them. Yet it could changed the lives of hundreds of thousands of Americans living in despair. I was encouraged.

Next I began buttonholing members of Congress for cosponsorship. I actually managed to sign on William Jefferson, Kweisi Mfume of Maryland, Charles Rangel, and Ed Towns, all members of the Congressional Black Caucus. On the Republican side, congressmen signed on rapidly. In a few weeks, the bill had fifty-eight original cosponsors—the most for any bill introduced by a freshman during the 102d Congress.

One member whose support I coveted was Newt Gingrich, then minority whip. I had been impressed with Gingrich's dedication and energy since the first day I saw him in action at the Republican Conference. Before the meeting began, Gingrich sat somewhat apart, shuffling through a pile of papers like a professor correcting a stack of midterm exams. "Hey, there's old Landslide Newt," said Conference Chairman Rep. Jerry Lewis (R-Cal.), greeting him. Gingrich had in fact won reelection by only 974 votes and the outcome was still in dispute. During the discussion that day I took special note to salute his leadership. "If you lived in my district, you would have won by a landslide," I said.

It took little time to garner Gingrich's support for the Urban Entrepreneurs Opportunity Act. One day I stopped him on the House floor and mentioned the proposal. "Put me down," he said tersely. With Gingrich and Minority Leader Bob Michel on board, the rest was easy.

Fred McClure, my White House contact, said the president would support the bill if two individuals were on board—Jack Kemp and Pat Saiki, the administrator of the Small Business Administration. I met with Kemp and he seemed interested if noncommittal. "I want to give it some thought," he said. I assured him it would not conflict with his own proposal for enterprise zones, but would enhance these zones since companies could invest without moving their own facilities into these areas. Pat Saiki also liked the idea.

Kemp got back in a few days and said he would support a

demonstration project that would test the idea in a target area before rolling it out nationwide. We said that was acceptable but would like to go to a nationwide effort as soon as possible.

Three weeks later we held an introductory press conference. Unfortunately—due to my naïveté—we bumped heads with the annual Congressional Art Contest, in which each House member submits a work of art from a high school student in his or her district. The contest always attracts the Capitol Hill press corps and our conference was attended by only a few Connecticut papers and an AP reporter. Questions from other congressmen focused around the affirmative action trade-offs. They feared the program would be purely "race-driven." I persisted that geography, not race, would be the major criterion.

Although I had enough cosponsors, the Democratic leadership refused to schedule hearings for what was being touted as a Republican bill. Hitting a stone wall in Congress, I decided to try piloting the idea in Connecticut. Lowell Weicker, although formerly a Republican, had become one of my chief antagonists. The conflict between the Weicker faction of the Connecticut GOP and the Rowland faction (to which I belonged) had finally split openly when Weicker was elected governor in 1990 while running as an independent. In addition, Weicker had veered much more toward the Democratic side. At a cocktail party attended by my sister-in-law Dolores Franks, who was Connecticut's deputy commissioner of health, Weicker had called me "an embarrassment to his race."

My meeting with Weicker was brief. Although we were both uncomfortable, Weicker agreed that if I could line up twenty-five companies each contributing one million dollars apiece, he would adjust Connecticut's tax structure to make the program beneficial to their interests. Unfortunately, neither of us ever followed up. Weicker began supporting my opponents by offering them the support of his independent party, the Connecticut Party. Our relationship quickly deteriorated, and I felt uncomfortable pursuing the idea any further.

Despite strong support, which grew to nearly one hundred cosponsors, the Urban Entrepreneurs Opportunity Act has never gotten a hearing in Congress. Even after the Republican victory of

1994, the 104th Congress has been so consumed with the nation's budget battles that there has not been time to deal with the issue. It is my fervent hope, however, that Congress will eventually have time to put the bill on the agenda—before the nation is once again consumed in urban violence.

My 1992 reelection was not easy. My 1990 win was regarded as such a fluke that everybody wanted to run against me. One candidate announced two months after I began my term in 1991. By mid-1992 there were eight candidates in the race—one of whom didn't even live in the district. I joked that people in the fifth district were walking into McDonald's saying, "I want a Big Mac with french fries and I'd like to run against Gary Franks."

"Okay. Next? "

"Give me a Quarter Pounder, large Coke, and I want to run against Gary Franks."

"No problem."

Over 70 percent of the mayors and selectmen in my district are Republican. Over 68 percent of the state senators are Republican. The district has not had a Democratic congressman since 1984 and has not voted Democratic in a presidential election since 1968. Yet people still seemed to feel that a black man representing a white district was a fluke and could be easily knocked off.

The Democratic field narrowed to two popular candidates: Jim Lawlor, a sixteen-year probate judge from Waterbury, and Lynn Taborsak, a woman plumber from Danbury who had served four terms in the state legislature. Taborsak was so popular among union members and feminists that she ended up on the cover of *Parade* magazine wearing her union helmet. Meanwhile, I was being touted as the legislative equivalent of Clarence Thomas.

Lawlor won the nomination at the party convention, but the vote was so close that Taborsak went on to a primary. The campaign was very nasty and Lawlor won again—but only by winning heavily among absentee voters from Waterbury, a result that some people found questionable. Once again, Taborsak decided not to give up.

Lowell Weicker—who by now was my sworn enemy—had won the governorship in 1990 as an independent. He now offered

Taborsak his Connecticut Party line, which would give her the top spot on the ballot.

Fortunately for me, the offer boomeranged. Lawlor was anti-abortion and ran poorly among conventional liberals. Taborsak picked up most of the defectors. They split the Democratic vote and I was declared the victor by 8:10 on election night. The final tabulation was Franks, 44 percent; Lawlor, 31 percent; Taborsak, 18 percent, with the remainder going to two other candidates. Together, my opponents spent close to a million dollars—far more than I spent to get reelected. My winning margin was thirty thousand votes. By midnight, people were once again lining up to run against me in 1994.

Once again, God had blessed me. I was in tune with my district, and I was ready for a second term. But things had changed radically. Bill Clinton had become the first Democratic president in twelve years. When I returned to Washington, the mood was entirely different.

ELEVEN

Racial Redistricting

WHEN I FIRST started attending Congressional Black Caucus meetings in 1991, the buzz was that the caucus would soon be expanding considerably. Everyone expected far more black members to be elected to Congress in 1992. I quickly learned that this was to be the result of racial gerrymandering. State legislatures redraw congressional district lines after the U.S. Census, which is conducted every tenth year. Redistricting is a regular event, and Republicans and Democrats always jockey to redraw the lines to their own party's advantage.

This time, however, things were to be different. In 1990, Democrats in Congress were arguing that the Voting Rights Act of 1964 required that blacks and Hispanics be represented by more blacks and Hispanics in Congress. The United States Civil Rights Commission weighed in and told states they would face lawsuits if the number of blacks and Hispanics did not increase.

As a black congressman representing a district that was 90 percent white, I was an embarrassment to all this finagling. I was living proof that blacks did not have to run in a majority-black district in order to get elected. If you represent what the voters really want, they will elect you whether you are black, brown, yellow, white, or any other color. The idea that only blacks could represent blacks and only whites could represent whites seemed an anathema to basic American principles.

Even more disturbing to me was a phone call I got from Ben Ginsberg, chief counsel for the Republican National Committee in late 1991. He wanted to alert me that major news organizations would probably be contacting me for comments on the creation of predominantly minority voting districts. I told Ginsberg I was strongly opposed to the idea of racial gerrymandering and assumed that this would be the Republican Party response.

"Actually we're not," said Ginsberg, surprising me. "It doesn't hurt us at all. In fact, it's probably going to help. With all the black and Hispanic votes concentrated in a few districts, it's going to be easier for us to win a lot of marginal districts that we've lost in the past."

"But that sounds like electoral homelands, like they have in South Africa," I told him.

"Look, the Democrats have been pushing this for years," said Ginsberg. "Let them have what they want."

Ginsberg's prediction proved true. In Georgia, as late as 1992, for example, Newt Gingrich was the only Republican in an eleven-member House delegation. Today, Georgia is represented by eight white Republicans and three black Democrats. Louisiana now has no white Democrats in Congress. By concentrating black representation, redistricting has disenfranchised white Democrats and has virtually wiped out the old Democratic Party.

In its own narrow terms, however, redistricting did prove successful. In 1992, voters elected forty black representatives to Congress—the largest number since Reconstruction. Instead of twenty-five to one, the vote was now likely to be thirty-nine to one in our Black Caucus meetings. The same election, of course, saw the triumph of Bill Clinton and the return of a Democrat to the White House for the first time in twelve years. The caucus was jubilant.

Our reception after the January swearing-in was so large that we had to hold it in the National Building Museum to accommodate the crowd. I must admit feeling an inescapable thrill as we boarded the bus from the Capitol and headed down Pennsylvania Avenue. All the new faces—from young Turks, such as Sanford Bishop of Georgia, to sixty-six-year-old Carrie Meek and Alcee Hastings, both of Florida—gave me a quiet excitement. I had never imagined being among so many black legislators. Everyone knew who I was, though, and left me alone in the middle of the bus.

The reception room at the museum was brimming with well-dressed men and women—and less well dressed radio and TV crews. U.S. Court of Appeals Judge Patrick Higginbotham administered the ceremonial swearing in of new CBC members. I could feel the older members trying to size up the new gang, even while relishing their new power. Many senior members also seemed surprised to see me back. They still considered my first election a fluke.

At the first meeting of the caucus, Rep. Kweisi Mfume of Maryland was elected our new chairman. An adept legislator and eloquent speaker who shared the caucus's views on social issues, Mfume was quietly suspicious of President Clinton and his "new Democrat" label. Few people had forgotten how Clinton distanced Jesse Jackson in the Sister Souljah incident during the campaign.

Our first guest speaker of the year was Reverend Jackson himself. The unofficial spokesman for black America had recently moved to Washington to serve as the District of Columbia's "shadow senator." Jackson told us our first order of business should be to achieve statehood for the District. Everyone—except me—agreed.

There seemed to be a certain amount of tension building between Jackson and the leaders of the CBC. Chairman Mfume showed Jackson a tremendous amount of respect, but after Jackson left, Rep. Earl Hilliard (D-Ala.) reminded everyone that the Reverend was not an elected official. "We're the ones who have the people's votes," he said.

Another early visitor to our lunchtime caucus was Hillary Rodham Clinton, the new First Lady. The first president's wife to visit the caucus, she proved to be a downright charming guest.

During the question-and-answer period, nearly everyone introduced themselves by talking about how hard they had worked to get her husband elected. Finally, I rose to ask a question about health care. Rep. Louis Stokes, chairman of the CBC's task force on health care reform, thought it necessary to jump in and explain, "This is our Republican member of the Congressional Black Caucus."

"I know who he is," said Mrs. Clinton.

"In contrast to everyone in this room," I told her, "I did not work hard to see you in this position. My district was your husband's worst in New England."

"Oh, I'm very well aware of that, too," she countered. Everyone got a good laugh.

The first month seemed like one continuous celebration. As winter wore on, however, the new members began to take on a more defensive posture. Many of their districts were now coming under court challenge. In *Shaw v. Reno,* the United States District Court in North Carolina had agreed to hear a suit against the state's Twelfth Congressional District, a particularly egregious example of gerrymandering. The district's boundaries included seventy-five miles of interstate highway connecting black populations in the cities of Charlotte and Winston-Salem. If you pulled off to a gas station by the side of the road you were in a new congressional district. As people became aware of the absurdity of this gerrymandering, objections began to be raised.

I made several speeches on the House floor expressing my belief that race should not be the predominant factor in the drawing of a congressional district. On June 30, 1993, I used the "one minute" rule at the start of each session to remark: "Mr. Speaker, we should not have laws that would give some Americans a manufactured advantage over other Americans. It would be wrong to favor white Americans and it is equally wrong to favor black Americans. All laws should be tailored to balance the scales of justice, not to tilt the scales, regardless of the alleged good intent."

The members of the CBC reacted to my speech as if it were a tear-gas grenade. Harold Ford, representative from Tennessee, caught me on the Capitol steps and said the entire CBC was mad at me. I asked why.

"Because of that one-minute remark you made today. You said something about districts being fixed so people could get elected. And you used a lot of Ivy Leaguish remarks to say it." He said the newly elected members were particularly incensed.

On the way back to my office in the Cannon House, I ran into Rep. Cleo Fields (D-La.), a freshman legislator with whom I had gotten along pretty well during the first few months of the year.

We took a long stroll on the Capitol lawn beneath the huge shade trees.

"Gary, I don't think we have to be enemies," he told me, "but I don't think we can agree on this issue."

I said I certainly didn't mean any personal attack toward him. I was sure he could get elected without any gerrymandering. I told him it just didn't seem like something in which black people should be involved—it would hurt us in the long run. He wasn't convinced, and as the conversation wore on it was clear we could only agree to disagree.

A few weeks later, I appeared on CNN's *Both Sides with Jesse Jackson*, broadcast out of Washington. During the debate, Jackson called me an "aberration" because I represented a mostly white district.

"Jesse, you must be an aberration, too," I shot back. "During your run for the presidency in 1988 you carried South Carolina, you carried my home state of Connecticut, and many, many other towns and cities with white majorities."

It was time for a station break, so Jackson only smiled at the camera and said, "I'll be back with my fellow aberration after this message."

Shortly afterward, I introduced a bill in the House making racially gerrymandered districts illegal. We quickly got one hundred Republican cosponsors—a number that typically ensures the bill will get a hearing in committee. But it never did. Not one Democrat would cosponsor the bill. Meanwhile, lawsuits had been filed challenging minority districts in Florida, Louisiana, Georgia, Texas, and North Carolina.

The Congressional Black Caucus countered by establishing a task force on redistricting. Cleo Fields served as chairman. Their first act was to solicit the help of the Justice Department. "I'm going to camp on Janet Reno's door if necessary," Cynthia McKinney (D-Ga.) told the CBC. A series of sixties-type rallies were scheduled for nearly every minority district affected.

One thing that impressed me was how much the Black Caucus was influenced by the writings of Lani Guinier, Bill Clinton's onetime nominee for assistant attorney general for civil rights. Guinier had developed an elaborate set of schemes that would give blacks voting power disproportionate to their numbers. One idea was to allow voters in at-large elections for city governments to cast all their votes for one candidate instead of voting for an entire slate. This way minority members could concentrate their votes and increase the chances of electing black candidates. She also argued that blacks had no real representation unless they were represented by "authentic" black people. It was truly news to me when I looked at myself in the mirror to realize that to some liberals I was not an authentic black.

All these ideas were soundly rejected when they became public. President Clinton quickly dumped Guinier and withdrew the nomination. Yet they lived on as a constant subject of discussion in the Congressional Black Caucus.

In mid-September, Cleo Fields came to the meeting of the CBC with good news. He had spoken with Deval Patrick, President Clinton's new nominee for the civil rights division, and had been assured that the administration would support racial redistricting.

About this time, I got a phone call from an attorney named Larry Chesin, who was representing the plaintiffs in a Georgia case against racial redistricting. It was Cynthia McKinney's district. Chesin knew about the legislation I had introduced and asked if I would testify in his case. McKinney's district stretched from Savannah to Atlanta, picking up pockets of black voters wherever it could. It was as if my district stretched from Danbury, Connecticut, to Boston, Massachusetts, picking up black neighborhoods in every city along the way.

I was reluctant to get involved in a case that didn't directly involve my constituents, although the repercussions of the case would affect legislative districts at all levels. The testimony was likely to be widely publicized and would only widen the rift between me and the Black Caucus. After talking it over with Donna and my chief of staff, Rick Genua, however, I decided it would enhance the chances of having my legislation adopted. The prospect of having black, brown, yellow, and white congressional districts was simply too appalling for me to sit back and do nothing. What do you tell youngsters in grade school when they say they would like to serve in Congress? "Go and find a district that matches your color"? That would be sad—and wrong.

At six months. Born February 9, 1953, in Waterbury, Connecticut, I was the sixth and youngest child (by nine years) of a very close family. (Courtesy of the author)

My parents, Jenary and Richard Franks. Anyone who visited our North End home in Waterbury could always count on a warm meal and a place to lay his or her head. As my mother would say, "A closed hand also allows nothing in." (Courtesy of the author)

My eighth-grade graduation photo from W. Tinker grade school. Since early childhood, education has always been of paramount importance in my family.

(Courtesy of the author)

When I first arrived at Yale University in 1971, I was intimidated by my high-caliber fellow students until I discovered that much of their success was the product of hard work and long nights in the university library. Here I am with my cousin Laura Chapman at my 1975 graduation. (Courtesy of the author)

The day Donna and I were married, March 10, 1990, was one of the happiest of my life. (Courtesy Charbonneau Photo, Watertown, CT)

Gary Jr., aged 1, getting his first taste of basketball with Dad. (Courtesy of the author)

On a short break in my Waterbury office with some of my support staff—my daughter Jessica and my son, Gary Jr.—in 1994. (Courtesy of the author)

The day after President Bush vetoed the 1990 civil rights bill, First Lady Barbara Bush was in Newton, Connecticut, attending a fund-raiser for me. (Courtesy of Barry Rubinowitz)

Former Vice President Dan Quayle has always been tremendously supportive of my work. After my first election, his fund-raiser helped me to set a personal record for campaign funds raised at a single event. (Courtesy of Barry Rubinowitz)

President George Bush with my extended family at my 1990 campaign fund-raiser. Left to right are my sister Joan; my niece Kendra; my sister-in-law Dolores; my mother, Jenary; me; my nephew Marvin Junior; my brother Richard Sylvester; my sister Bonita; my sister Ruth; and my brother Marvin. (Courtesy of Barry Rubinowitz)

Then–First Lady Barbara Bush, my chief of staff, part-time campaign manager, and long-time friend, Rick Genua, and I enjoy a few laughs at the annual White House picnic.
(Courtesy of the White House)

Dr. Henry Kissinger has been one of my strongest supporters over the years. At my campaign fund-raiser in 1991, I gave him a map of the fifth district as a memento.

(Courtesy of Barry Rubinowitz)

In 1994, I announced my candidacy for Congress. Pictured here with my daughter Jesica and State Senator Stephen Somma.

(Courtesy of the author)

The critical importance of education and the power of youth can not be overstated. I frequently visit schools and community centers to speak with young people about their goals and aspirations. Here I am at the Shelton-Derby Boys and Girls Club in Shelton, Connecticut. (Courtesy of the author)

When I was a freshman representative in 1990, the Congressional Black Caucus attempted to throw me out when my views on some issues differed from theirs. Pictured here, the 103rd Congressional Black Caucus (from the bottom of the stairs to the top, then to the left, and finally those near the railing): Harold Ford, Carol Moseley-Braun, Kweisi Mfume, Alan Wheat, Cardiss Collins, Maxine Waters, Barbara Rose-Collins, Alcee Hastings, Bobby Scott, Corrine Brown, Jim Cliburn, Carrie Meek, Donald Payne, Cynthia McKinney, Bennie Thompson, Major Owens, Eleanor Holmes Norton, Louis Stokes, Julian Dixon, Ed Towns, Bill Jefferson, me, Earl Hilliard, Mel Reynolds, Mel Watt, Cleo Fields, Charles Rangel, Sanford Bishop, Albert Wynn, Ron Dellums, Floyd Flake, Eva Clayton, John Lewis, Lucien Blackwell. (Courtesy of the Congressional Black Caucus Foundation)

In 1992, I was deeply honored to address the Republican National Convention.

(Courtesy of the author)

overnor John Engler of Michigan presenting
e with the state's Frederick Douglass Award
1994. (Courtesy of Fred Ferris)

I look forward to working with Senator Bob
Dole to help him become our next president.
His emphasis on inclusion, on "one America,"
is a goal that I too embrace. (Courtesy of the author)

have the utmost respect and admiration for General Colin Powell, pictured here in 1991 with
yself and Representative Ed Towns (center). (Courtesy of the U.S. House of Representatives)

President Bill Clinton and I greet one another at the annual White House picnic. (Courtesy of the White House)

Family has always been central in my life and a source of great strength. I am grateful to have been blessed with my wonderful wife, Donna; my daughters Jessica, aged 3½, and Azia, aged 10; and my son, Gary Jr., aged 6 months. (Courtesy of the author)

A few days later, while walking through the Capitol basement, I ran into David Lightman, a reporter for the *Hartford Courant*. During our discussion I mentioned I would be testifying in the Georgia case. The story made not only the *Courant* but the *Washington Post*. The following day, I started receiving numerous messages on my answering machine from leaders of the NAACP advising me not to go to Georgia. Some of them were quite threatening and warned I would pay for it if I followed through. (I later informed the FBI of these threats.) I decided to go anyway.

Rick and I flew from Hartford to Savannah. The plaintiffs drove us to the hotel in a rented Lincoln Continental—which caused us considerable embarrassment. We were mildly concerned about our safety and, like characters in *Mission: Impossible*, covertly switched hotel rooms after we registered.

Somehow I felt the black waiters and waitresses who served us breakfast the next morning knew exactly what I was doing in Georgia and were reproaching me for it. I wanted to tell them I hoped they understood I was trying to foster good race relations, not deprive them of black congressional representation.

Our guide to the courthouse turned out to be a young white woman. Now my paranoia switched back the other way. I was glad that Rick was with us so I wouldn't be suspected of escorting a white lady around the streets of Savannah. I also became mildly suspicious when she said she couldn't accompany us into the courthouse because she had to park the car. Was it that she didn't want to be seen with me? To add to the day's distractions, Rick and I got lost trying to find the courtroom.

When we finally arrived, I immediately saw a familiar face—Rep. Corrine Brown from Florida, who frequently took the trouble to move away from me at Black Caucus lunch meetings. Her district had been gerrymandered and she would be affected by the outcome of this case. When she saw me enter, Brown turned and stared coldly into my eyes. If looks could kill, I would have been dead. I took a seat about three rows behind the plaintiff's attorneys. Larry Chesin saw me and quickly motioned me into a small anteroom. It was the first time I had actually met him. He seemed bright and articulate.

"Can you be available to answer questions for the press after your testimony?" he asked. I said I would. He then went over the basics of the case. "Oh, one more thing," he added. "There may be a few members of the press outside after you're finished. Are you ready for that?" I said everything was all right as long as I didn't miss my plane back to Washington.

While walking back into the courtroom, I asked Woody Lovell, McKinney's Republican opponent and one of the two plaintiffs, how the case was going.

"Fine." He smiled. "Two of the judges will probably go with us. The other is hopeless."

"Let's not get overconfident," interrupted Chesin. "Anything can happen. The final arbiter on this case will probably be the U.S. Supreme Court."

I went back to sit among the spectators. A casual glance told me that neither Congresswoman McKinney nor any other member of the Georgia delegation was present. I also recognized Clyde Murphy, whom I had met at a meeting of the Yale University Black Alumni in New York. Murphy had used that occasion to lambaste me publicly for my conservative views. Several people told me later they were embarrassed by the way he had turned a friendly gathering into a political confrontation. Now he was with the NAACP Legal and Educational Defense Fund. I expected the worst from his cross-examination.

As I sat listening, witnesses for the plaintiffs argued that one or two of the current congressional representatives had literally carved their own districts while sitting in the Georgia state legislature in 1991. They also noted that the legislatures had been unwilling to settle for simple majorities of fifty-five to forty-five. Congresswoman McKinney's district was given a 64 percent black majority in order to offset traditionally low black turnout.

Then it was my turn. As I took the witness chair, the judges greeted me cordially, and the two defense attorneys representing Georgia smiled at me.

At first the questions were routine. Then they asked me to comment on Congresswoman McKinney's testimony. It appeared she had been unable to identify some of the towns and counties in her own district.

"It would be difficult for me to represent any community in my district if I didn't know its name," I said.

Then Clyde Murphy arose for cross-examination. I expected the worst but quickly realized he didn't feel nearly as confident confronting me in the courtroom as he had been berating me in front of fellow Yale alumni.

"What percent of the vote did you get in your 1992 reelection?" he asked.

"About forty-four percent," I said.

"Isn't it true that you had the lowest winning percentage of any congressional candidate in the last election?"

"It was an unusual situation. There were five candidates. I won twenty-five of twenty-seven municipalities and finished thirteen percentage points ahead of the second-place candidate."

"Are you here representing the Black Caucus?"

"No."

"How many members of the Congressional Black Caucus, other than yourself, were elected from districts in which blacks were not a majority? "

"I believe a number of the representatives were initially elected in districts where blacks were not a majority. I believe Alan Wheat of Missouri, Ron Dellums of California, Harold Ford of Tennessee, and Mike Espy of Mississippi all represent districts in which blacks were not a majority."

I was wrong about Espy, and Murphy pounced on my mistake. He noted that the courts had stepped in to assure that Espy would run in a district that was over 50 percent black. "Thanks to the courts, Mike Espy has been given a true opportunity to become a congressman." In the end, he sounded more like the Clyde Murphy I remembered from New York.

One of the judges asked me about the importance of "common interest" in the makeup of a congressional district.

"You don't have to be black in order to represent black people any more than you have to be white in order to represent white people," I replied. "We should not see districts as being black or white but as being American districts with the prevailing interest in what's best for the local communities and the country. My election by a nearly all-white constituency is proof that color is not the key ingredient in representation."

The judges thanked me and I was dismissed.

As I left the courtroom, Woody Lowell, the losing candidate for Congress, caught me and warned me there was a "small demonstration" going on outside.

"What exactly do you mean, a 'small demonstration'?" I asked.

"About a dozen people are marching back and forth carrying picket signs."

"Gary, Billy McKinney, the congresswoman's father, is outside there," Chesin warned me. "He's pretty high-spirited. Be prepared."

I said I would be.

Meanwhile, I had to meet the press. Several reporters commented that I did not live in the South and therefore couldn't really understand racism. I had probably never really experienced it living in the North either. I said my family was from North Carolina and mentioned that the Ku Klux Klan once burned a cross on my family's lawn. The three plaintiff attorneys stood directly behind me, trying to appear on camera. The irony of a group of white reporters telling a black man he didn't understand racism seemed lost on everyone.

As we finally made our way out the front corridor, I caught sight of the protesters. It looked like far more than a dozen people. They were all black. As the courthouse door swung open, the cameramen and photographers scrambled to get a good angle.

The signs bore messages: GARY FRANKS IS AN UNCLE TOM and FRANKS GO HOME! At the bottom of the stairs, a strangely familiar gentleman was waiting with his arms extended. He sported a MCKINNEY FOR CONGRESS sweatshirt. I realized this was Billy McKinney. I had met him briefly during our swearing-in party in January. I did not realize at the time that he was also a state representative in the Georgia legislature.

As I reached the bottom of the stairs, McKinney reached out and shook my hand. Then he started screaming in my ear. "Did you have a nice time in there, Gary? Did you have fun selling the brothers out? What did they give you, you nigger? You're a black Judas. Why don't you fight me like a man?"

Rick and I tried to move forward as McKinney kept clutching my hand. I finally yanked loose.

I turned around and found my three white escorts, the plaintiffs, and the police officer had all disappeared. It was just Rick and me. We stared straight ahead and marched for what seemed to be about a mile to where we were to meet the car. Miraculously, the Lincoln Continental had been transformed into a two-door Camaro—although at this point I think I would have preferred a tank. I squeezed into the back while Billy McKinney continued to shout at me through the window. My last recollection of Savannah was three television camera lenses staring at me like blind robots while all around demonstrators screamed and Billy McKinney jumped up and down like a wild man.

TWELVE

~~~

A Visit to the White House: Tired Feet, Rested Soul

T HE CONGRESSIONAL Black Caucus took great exception to my Georgia testimony. "You should learn to stay out of other people's districts," Rep. Cardiss Collins of Illinois told me when we met on the floor of the House.

The *Hartford Courant* ran a front-page story saying the Connecticut NAACP would oppose me in the next election. Since I was a longtime member of the NAACP, some of my dues would actually be spent to fund my own opposition. When I walked onto the floor the next day, Maxine Waters was handing out copies of the story. "Look what your home state paper is saying about you," she hissed, brandishing the headline. "You should be ashamed of yourself."

When Bernard Goldberg of CBS's *Eye to Eye* asked Waters on camera, "Let me ask you about Gary Franks," she snapped, "I don't know him."

"Yes, she does," Goldberg informed viewers. "What Congresswoman Waters is saying is that she doesn't *want* to know him."

At the CBC lunch meetings, the subject of racial districts occupied more and more of the agenda. Federal district courts in North Carolina and Louisiana were already overturning the new districts, and it looked as if the whole matter was headed for the Supreme Court. Cynthia McKinney was on the agenda to report on her case at one point but refused to do so in my presence. The following week, Cleo Fields said we should try to get the Supreme Court to delay its decision until 1995 so it would not affect the 1994 congressional elections.

After Fields had spoken, I got up and gave a speech.

"You know, the Republican Party is getting ready to run twenty-five black candidates for Congress next year, very few of them in gerrymandered districts. J. C. Watts is being given a very good chance of winning in Oklahoma. Ron Freeman is running in Missouri. I'm not even the only black Republican candidate in Connecticut anymore. Susan Johnson, a Columbia law school graduate, is going to take on a two-term Democratic incumbent. Ken Blackwell, who lost for Congress in Cincinnati, has been appointed state treasurer and will be seeking a full term. Vikki Buckley has a good chance of winning secretary of state in Colorado. It seems to me this strategy of going mainstream is eventually going to produce a lot more black elected officials than racial gerrymandering."

There was an embarrassed silence. Finally, Alcee Hastings of Florida spoke up: "What in the world do the comments of the gentleman from Connecticut have to do with what Mr. Fields was talking about?"

The following week, the three-judge panel in Georgia voted two to one that the drawing of congressional districts to ensure racial representation was unconstitutional. Its ruling was subsequently upheld by the U.S. Supreme Court. Many states are now being forced to redraw their lines again in order to eliminate racial gerrymandering.

A few months after my trip to Savannah, Billy McKinney had contacted my office and said he wanted to apologize for his actions outside the courthouse. I resisted a meeting at first but finally saw

him for a few minutes in the presence of Rick Genua and Cynthia
McKinney. He told me of the discrimination he had suffered over
the years. When he began his career as a police officer, he said, he
had been immediately instructed to arrest only black people. He
was not allowed to arrest white people. I told him I admired his
efforts, and we parted on reasonably good terms.

A few months later, it became clear why McKinney had been
anxious to make amends. Rick Genua and I were visited by two
FBI agents who were investigating the confrontation outside the
courthouse. One of the judges had seen tapes of the incident on
the evening news and wanted the U.S. attorney's office to bring
charges.

McKinney was eventually brought to trial for contempt of
court just before the Christmas holidays in 1993. Rick went down
to testify as the prosecution's sole witness. McKinney essentially
pleaded guilty and brought only character witnesses to recount
his long public service. He was convicted and fined five hundred
dollars, the minimum penalty. Amazingly, while on the witness
stand, Cynthia McKinney testified that she was the only person in
the Black Caucus who had ever treated me as a human being.

The day after the verdict, I ran into Mac Collins, one of the
growing number of Republicans in the Georgia delegation. He
knew all about the case and congratulated me on my handling of
the incident. Yet once again, he reiterated the Republicans' dual
purposes on the whole issue. "Quite frankly, the redistricting has
helped us," he told me. "It creates a few sure-black districts, but it
makes every other district a little easier to win."

Texas Republican Sam Johnson, who represents Dallas, told me
the same thing. "I used to visit all the black churches and take a lot
of concern for minority voters because they were part of my constituency," he said. "Now I'm in a district that is almost all white. I
just don't worry about black people as much as I once did." It's a
sad statement that we have created this type of polarization.

Despite these logistics, Collins, Gingrich, and Louisiana
Republicans Richard Baker and Jim McCrery all cosponsored my
bill to eliminate racial gerrymandering. I admired them for putting
the national interest ahead of their own reelection strategies.

*   *   *

As 1993 wore on, my relations with the Black Caucus continued to deteriorate. The first sign of trouble was at our regular Wednesday luncheon meetings. My mere presence seemed to disturb some of the members. Rep. Earl Hilliard muttered one day, "Should we be discussing these strategies before this Republican member?" Other members looked at each other, not knowing whether or not it would be appropriate to ask me to leave the room.

After a few weeks of such tensions, Hilliard offered a motion by which the Congressional Black Caucus would dissolve itself into the CBC Democratic Caucus and hold an executive session without me. Another member seconded the motion. Chairman Mfume asked for but received no discussion. The caucus then voted to transform itself into a Democrats-only body. I gathered my materials and headed for the door. CBC Executive Director Amelia Parker came running after me and said, almost apologetically, "I don't think this will happen often. They just want to talk about some things that are strategic in nature."

"It's OK with me," I told her.

Soon it became routine. Like clockwork, after our thirty-minute luncheon, someone would offer a motion that the caucus dissolve itself into a Democrats-only body. After the first time, no one bothered to apologize. Yet I still got the distinct feeling that some of the senior members felt uncomfortable with the procedure. They knew they were risking the caucus's nonpartisan status.

Not all our luncheon meetings involved strategy. At one point we were treated to a visit by Secretary of Labor Robert Reich, who sounded as if he had replaced Monty Hall as host of *Let's Make a Deal*. After making a point of how much President Clinton needed the caucus's support, Reich went on to show how the administration's job training bill would include a sizable chunk of federal dollars that would be disbursed to each and every Black Caucus member's district.

I saw the members' eyes turning into dollar signs as they contemplated just how much money this program was going to bring home. I got so caught up in it myself that I was almost tempted to ask what the figures would be for my district. I had to snap myself out of this trance by reminding myself that all this was other people's money we were spending.

The CBC's meeting with Donna Shalala, secretary of health and human services, was in the same vein. She informed us how, after months of foot-dragging, the Clinton administration was putting forth a proposal on how to end "welfare as we know it"— as the president had promised so eloquently during his campaign.

Needless to say, the plan was nothing but another expansion of government's efforts to baby-sit the poor rather than an incentive for private effort or personal responsibility. Although the stated purpose was to limit welfare dependency, it was obvious that the bill was only going to increase dependency.

During the question period, I asked Shalala whether, despite the legislation's stated purposes, it would still be possible for recipients to stay on welfare for more than two years.

"Yes," she said, "under certain circumstances." She went on for about two minutes, listing virtually every imaginable circumstance: people who have looked for work and can't find any, people who need training, women who have additional children, people who have disabilities, people whose children have disabilities or require special attention, and on and on and on.

"So," I asked, "under certain circumstances, people can probably stay on welfare their entire lives?"

"Yes," she answered sheepishly.

The Clinton administration's initial efforts at "reinventing" welfare were about as modern as slapping a fresh coat of paint on a stagecoach.

After many months of these introductory skirmishes, however, the big day finally arrived—an invitation for the caucus to visit the White House for a meeting with the president. For the newer members, this represented a triumphant affirmation of their own victories and a chance to celebrate the return of the presidency to Democratic hands. "This is the end of a long, uphill road for the Democratic Party," said one of the members.

"No, this is going to be a meeting between the president and the entire Congressional Black Caucus," Chairman Mfume corrected him. "Mr. Franks will be there, too."

Mel Reynolds, my old basketball recruit from Yale, now representing Illinois, rolled his eyes in exasperation.

In fact, with the Democrats in control of both Congress and

the White House, the caucus didn't seem to need me much anymore. When George Bush was president, it had been useful for them to maintain contacts with the other side. But now Republicans seemed outclassed and irrelevant. Close to half the members of the caucus had contributed to my opponent's campaign during the 1994 congressional election. I had become little more than a nuisance.

With the repeated insult of being asked to leave at every other meeting, I finally came to a momentous decision: I would resign my seat on the caucus. I talked it over with my wife, family members, and chief of staff. It seemed ridiculous to spend five thousand dollars a year of taxpayers' money to belong to a group that didn't do anything but allow me to eat lunch with them once a week. In June 1993, I called a Monday news conference and asked my press secretary, Jeff Muthersbuagh, to write up a press release announcing my intention to resign from the caucus.

By the weekend, my impending break was big news throughout the Nutmeg State. The story made radio, newspapers, and television. My home answering machine overflowed with messages, nearly all of them urging me to stick it out. I attended functions throughout my district over the weekend, and everywhere I went people urged me to hang in there. "Don't quit," they protested. "It's not your style."

In fact, the two reasons people gave against my resigning made sense. First, they said if my membership irritated the Congressional Black Caucus so much, I might be doing something right. The group itself tended to be very claustrophobic and took positions that were extreme, even for liberal Democrats. Second, they said, whether I realized it or not, I was doing a lot to improve race relations. Although it was tough to be the point man, somebody had to be out there taking the heat if things were to improve in American society.

By Sunday evening I had to acknowledge they were right. Resigning from the caucus would only take pressure off the members and allow them to become even more extreme. It was a ticklish situation. My press release was already printed. Yet until I actually stepped up to a bank of microphones, nothing had changed.

On Monday morning, at a well-attended press conference, I

surprised the fifty or so reporters by stating that I would *not* resign from the Congressional Black Caucus. I explained to the packed house that I wanted to play a continuing role in improving U.S. race relations in America. I also noted that if I so consistently aggravated liberal Democrats in Congress, then I must be doing something right.

As soon as the conference ended, my office started receiving calls of congratulations. There were also a few urgent messages from Black Caucus members. Some didn't believe the news that I was going to stick with it, others were expressing their disappointment. At the next meeting, however, no one acted any differently than they had before my attempted resignation.

On July 21, 1993, the Congressional Black Caucus boarded a bus at the Capitol steps and started down Pennsylvania Avenue for a trip to see President Clinton. The visit had been long planned. Just before we left, I had asked Chairman Mfume if I would be able to ask a question. He just stared right through me and didn't say a thing.

People had gotten into the habit of edging away from me whenever seating arrangements were made. Now I realized the same thing was going to happen on the bus. Should I just take a seat in the back and allow myself to be isolated? No. I decided I was going to take a seat smack in the middle of the bus. Let people arrange themselves around me however they wished. Sure enough, when everybody had settled down, there was a cordon of empty seats around me.

As the bus lurched through traffic, I reflected on how many black people had been in my situation before me. I thought about Rosa Parks sitting in the back of the bus for so many years and then suddenly refusing to give up her seat. "My feet are tired, but my soul is rested," she had said. I wondered what she would think of me now. My basketball legs still felt great, but my spirit was uneasy. How many black people had sat like this, shunned by their own people?

Then again, I thought, what's the difference? God never gives you any more than you can handle. I might be the most unpopular person on the bus, but I was still right smack in the middle of the nation's capital, going to meet the president. How many people could have that as part of their day?

At the White House, we followed a carefully choreographed script. We were to discuss a few common concerns and then move on so as not to disrupt the president's busy schedule. Probably only a few people would get to speak. By the way several members rushed to get to the front seats, I realized everyone else had a question to ask the president.

The first person I recognized inside the White House was presidential spokesman George Stephanopolous. I had seen him several times on the House floor working with Majority Leader Dick Gephardt. He nodded to me as we crowded into the Roosevelt Room looking for seats. I sat down next to Corrine Brown. As soon as she noticed me, she stood up and moved to another chair.

The president was at the front of the room with Vice President Al Gore on his right. Mr. Clinton was much taller than I expected but looked very tired. Although an imposing figure, he seemed a bit distracted. Only hours before, his close friend and deputy counsel Vincent Foster had apparently committed suicide in a suburban park. Chairman Mfume thanked the president for meeting with us only hours after the tragedy.

The president spoke softly. He said he was very distressed over Foster's death but thought it was essential to keep our appointment because of the importance of the Black Caucus in the enormous tasks that lay ahead of us. He admired the work of the Black Caucus and felt that it was the nation's conscience, playing a special role in leading us toward becoming a more just society. Then he turned the meeting over to Representative Mfume.

The chairman called on Rep. John Conyers, who asked an elaborate question relating to health care. The president responded briefly. Then a few more people asked questions to the same effect. Vice President Gore did not say a word but sat listening intently to everything that was said.

I decided to put up my hand. Mfume ignored me and called on someone else. The same thing happened several times. Finally, he looked directly into my eyes . . . and called on someone else again.

"I would like to thank you, Mr. President, for having this meeting with us today," he finished. "It's been very cordial of you to allow us to express some of our concerns, particularly under these circumstances."

That's when I stood up. As I did, several security people grabbed for their chests. They probably weren't feeling indigestion. "Mr. President, Mr. President . . ." I said forcefully.

"Yes, Gary," the president responded. Everyone—including me—was surprised that he knew my name.

"Mr. President," I began, "if this is truly a Congressional Black Caucus meeting, then I—as the only Republican member—should be allowed to address you with a question or a comment."

"Mr. President, Mr. Franks is totally out of order here," interrupted Mfume.

"That's all right," said the president. "I have no problem. I'd like to hear what Gary has to say." Through the corner of my eye, I saw the security detail easing up a bit.

"Mr. President, I may have more in common with you than many of the members in this room may believe," I began. "I agree with you that you need a line-item veto, similar to what you had as governor of Arkansas. I agree with you that we need a balanced budget amendment as you had when you were governor. I support you on NAFTA. I agree with your efforts to end welfare as we know it. Unwed motherhood is one of the great problems in this country, and we need greater efforts in identifying the fathers of illegitimate children. I look forward to working with you on that.

"Where I disagree with you, Mr. President, is in the interpretation of the Voting Rights Act, which says that we need to create special minority election districts. I don't think it is necessary to manufacture the results of elections. I believe that the people of this country have enough common interests so that race should not be the deciding factor in drawing congressional election districts."

As I finished, the entire caucus was staring at me like a pack of alley cats.

The president said he agreed with most of my comments and appreciated my support. Where he differed strongly was on the Voting Rights Act. He said that the long history of discrimination in America made it necessary to take remedial measures and that the whole country was served better if black people were allowed to elect blacks to Congress.

Seeing that no one had anything to add, the president closed the meeting by saying he had enjoyed it and hoped we could meet regularly.

As the meeting ended, many caucus members rushed forward to shake the president's hand and exchange a few remarks. I also tried to get close, but several members positioned their bodies to keep me away. Staff members slowly began guiding the president out of the room. I persisted, however, and a minute later I found myself eye-to-eye with the commander in chief.

I thanked him for his comments and reiterated my view that it was unnecessary to create minority districts in order to get blacks elected to Congress. "I come from a ninety percent white district," I said. "I'm living proof." As we spoke, members listened as if it were one of those old E.F. Hutton ads.

When I mentioned welfare reform, the president pointed to David Gergen, his recently appointed aide, and suggested I follow up with him. Several other caucus members intervened and I left. As I started down the aisle, I literally collided with Gergen, an imposing six-foot-five figure who towered over me. I mentioned the president's remarks. "I look forward to working with you," he said. "On welfare we need bipartisan support." We promised to keep in touch.

As we walked toward the bus, I heard people talking about me.

"I told you we should have dealt with this long ago," Bill Clay whispered to Mel Reynolds.

"Don't worry," responded Reynolds. "We'll fix him at lunch."

On the ride back up Pennsylvania Avenue, I truly felt like the invisible man of the old Jim Crow South. I sat amidst a bus full of people who literally wished I would just disappear. As noontime shoppers strolled on downtown avenues and people sunned themselves on the Capitol Mall, I wondered what the caucus had in store for me at our luncheon meeting.

THIRTEEN

~∞~

Blacklisted

Y ou spoke out of order," Chairman Mfume scolded me even before the caucus had reassembled for lunch.

"I asked to speak before going to the White House and you didn't answer," I reminded him. "I just assumed that, time permitting, I could make my comments to the president."

None of this soothed the nerves of caucus members. Mfume stared at me in silence.

"I think we should do what I felt should have been done a long time ago," Mel Reynolds stated matter-of-factly as the members settled into their chairs. "It's very clear, Gary, that we are not pleased with you. We do not feel comfortable with you in our presence and, quite frankly, you may not feel comfortable in our presence either. There are major differences between us. I personally believe it's time for a parting of the ways."

Louis Stokes, a senior member from Ohio, interrupted and warned Reynolds, "Before you say that, I think we should have a little dialogue on what we're getting ready to do because I think that this represents a significant step. We've never done anything like this before."

Eva Clayton of North Carolina added, "I'd like to hear from some of the more senior members on this subject."

I sat there listening as the members went back and forth over what they were prepared to do. I was seated between Floyd Flake of New York and Bobby Rush of Illinois, two of the more decent members who had always treated me with respect. They both looked very uncomfortable. Slowly it dawned on me that everyone was preparing to expel me this very afternoon.

After a few more people made points, Charles Rangel, the veteran from New York, spoke up. "We are about to make Mr. Franks much bigger than he is today," he warned. "We are going to make him into a martyr. You newer members may not realize it, but he's going to be much more famous outside the caucus than he ever was in it." You could hear a pin drop.

Louis Stokes turned to me. "Gary, I want to hear from you on this. Why do you want to be in this organization? You don't seem to fit our philosophical perspective."

"It's ironic to me," I began, "that the person who is making the motion to expel me here is somebody whom I've known since I was nineteen years old. I helped recruit Mel Reynolds to Yale University. I was asked by the basketball coach to take him in for the weekend and sell him on the school. Apparently I did a good job. I helped give him the opportunity to get a great education and you're the one leading the move to treat me in this manner." Reynolds refused to meet my gaze.

I began to get rather emotional. "During all my years as a college student I admired the Black Caucus. I still admire it. It has truly served as a conscience for this country. I may differ with you on many issues, but I don't think being different is wrong or bad. I have the same goals as you do, to improve the lives of African Americans and Americans in general. Yes, we differ on how to get there. But that doesn't make either of us any less desirous of reaching those goals."

Mfume went around the room asking each member to comment. Each one had a favorite Gary Franks story. They rehearsed things I had said on the floor of the House, votes I had cast, off-the-cuff comments I had made. When I tried to respond, Mfume cut me off. "You've already had your chance to talk," he snapped. On and on they went. I had consistently voted against the interests of the poor in general and African Americans in particular. They found my position on the Voting Rights Act indefensible. It went on endlessly.

Finally, I was given the opportunity to say a few more words. I replied to Eleanor Holmes Norton's charges that I never supported her legislative agenda.

"Eleanor, I've supported you on many issues, as you well know. I've been one of the strongest supporters in the Republican Party on District of Columbia funding." Looking at Louis Stokes, I said, "Lou, I can point to a number of votes on which you and I have agreed on things." (I had supported him on Veterans Administration, HUD, Department of Labor, and Health and Human Services appropriations bills.)

The others protested once again. The meeting dragged on and on. Eventually I left for a vote in the House chamber.

Late that afternoon, I ran into Kenneth Cooper of the *Washington Post* in the Speaker's press area just behind the House rostrum. "What's your response to the action the Black Caucus took against you today?" he asked.

"I have no idea what happened," I said.

After I left, he informed me, they had tabled Mel Reynolds's motion to expel me but had passed a motion by Alcee Hastings requiring me to leave each session after the thirty-minute lunch. Rather than having to vote on my departure at every meeting, it would become the rule.

"As long as I'm still a member of Congress, they'll be hearing from me," I told Cooper.

At our next meeting, Chairman Mfume began by announcing that every Wednesday the noon meeting would adjourn at 12:30 sharp. At that point, Mfume would turn the gavel over to CBC Vice Chairman Cardiss Collins (D-Ill.), who would preside over a meeting of the Democratic Congressional Black Caucus. When the DCBC dissolved, the gavel would return to Mfume and I would be allowed to return.

As the clock ticked closer to 12:30 P.M., I was still eating my lunch. Charles Rangel smiled and said, "Let him have his pie and ice cream before he leaves." Everyone chuckled.

"I bet he doesn't have chocolate ice cream on top of his apple pie," chortled Brooklyn's Major Owens. The laughter grew louder.

"I'll pass on both," I said and quickly departed. Outside a couple of reporters and a TV camera crew were waiting for me to emerge.

"What happened?" Alan McConagha of the *Washington Times* asked me.

"They told me to have my lunch and leave."

"What did you have for lunch?" he asked.

"Chicken."

"They told you to have your chicken and leave?"

"They told me to have my chicken and leave."

It had a nice ring to it. The quote appeared in several newspapers.

A few days later, Rep. Bill Clay, one of the most uncompromising of the senior members, sent me a thirteen-page "open letter" laying out our differences and detailing the charges against me. He wrote,

> It is incumbent upon me to reiterate my opposition to your insensitivity to and callous disregard for the basic rights and freedoms of 35 million black Americans. To remain silent any longer may at a future time imperil the well-being of black Americans. . . . Your Byzantine ideas supporting the denial of the resources of government to enhance opportunities for black people to compete on a par with others speaks volumes about the ability of a few institutions of higher learning to mesmerize the reasoning process of some highly intelligent individuals. Of course, it is your prerogative to vote the will of your "95% white constituency" as you constantly remind us. But, Sir, 35 million black Americans that your votes adversely impact must also live with the consequences of your action. . . . [I]n my opinion, it would probably be better for all concerned if you did resign [from the CBC] forthwith, admitting you never should have joined the ranks of black legislators who fight to protect the rights of black people. . . . I offer [this material] in the hope of jarring your psyche to the reality that black is black and white is white and never the twain shall meet.

Comments from other members were in the same vein.

Media interest began to grow. I was interviewed on Pat Buchanan's radio program. About the same time, my office got a call from the *Rush Limbaugh Show*. His producer, James Golden, who is black, had read the stories and was stunned by the caucus's behavior. Limbaugh had me on shortly after.

"Is it true," Limbaugh began, "that the members of the Black Caucus have told you to have your lunch—eat your chicken—and leave? They let you stay a half hour and then you have to go?"

I walked him through the history of the conflict. Then he asked, "Well, why do you want to be in a group like that anyway?"

"I believe in dialogue," I responded. "Contrasting your ideas with someone else's is healthy. Sometimes you change your mind or change someone else's. That's the purpose of our whole representative system of government. The caucus would be the first to cry foul if they learned that George Bush belonged to an all-white country club, yet they cannot tolerate the presence of me—one different voice—in their own councils."

My interview with Limbaugh lasted less than fifteen minutes. Yet to this day, anywhere I go in this country, someone will come up to me and say, "I remember hearing you on Rush's show."

After that appearance, faxes began cascading into Congress. CBC administrator Amelia Parker and other members received phone calls denouncing the Black Caucus for what people called a new form of bigotry. Overwhelmed by the grassroots reaction, Parker rang my office. "Please call them off!" she pleaded. "Rush Limbaugh's people are inundating us. Tell them to stop!"

The *Wall Street Journal* published three editorials supporting me. One chided the Black Caucus for treating me as "$\frac{3}{5}$ of a member," a reference to the constitutional compromise that counted slaves as "three-fifths of all other Persons." The publicity could not have come at a worse time for them. The Congressional Black Caucus Foundation, the CBC's nonprofit educational organization, was preparing for its annual fund-raising dinner at which it regularly solicits millions of dollars from the business community. As a result of my ouster, many contributors were threatening to reduce their donations.

Money troubles aside, Charles Rangel's prediction was ringing loud and clear. Expelling me had given me much greater public attention than I had ever received while sitting in the caucus's meetings. A few days later, Mfume called my office. "Look, we've got to get this worked out," he said. "I don't know why these newer members have such a problem with you. The senior members may disagree with you, but we have no problem with you attending our meetings. I think these newer members now realize they have made a mistake. I hear you're preparing a lawsuit."

In fact, I was. "I've obtained a copy of the charter," I told him. "It says specifically that the CBC is a *bi*-partisan organization. There is no reference to anything called the Democratic Congressional Black Caucus. I think I've got a good case against you."

"Well, look, let's get this thing behind us," said Mfume. "What do we have to do?"

"Let's have a news conference and let people know you changed your mind."

"Look, do this," Mfume suggested. "Put down the things you have to have and we'll see what we can do."

"Are you agreeing to a news conference?"

"Yes, I agree to a news conference. I think I can get the caucus to go along. They know in principle they have to get away from the 'have lunch and you're gone' routine. There may be times when you can't be present, but we can't have this attitude that you shouldn't be in there with us."

"I'll write down what I feel I have to have and we'll shoot for a news conference right away," I agreed. "We can have one today if you want."

"Well, let me see what I can pull together."

I jotted down a few comments that captured my feelings about the issue. I also prepared a few words for Representative Mfume to tell the press. In a few moments, they were being faxed to his office in the Rayburn Building.

In order to hold a conference in the House Radio and TV Gallery, you must be sponsored by a broadcast media organization. I wanted the news conference to happen right away, so I called Phyllis Crockett of National Public Radio. Although NPR's slant is strictly liberal, Crockett had recently interviewed me and I thought she might be willing to help. Sure enough, she came through, and before you knew it, we were set for the next day.

Mfume was stunned that we were able to arrange a press conference so quickly. As Rick Genua said, he looked as if he were being led to the slaughter. I can't say I envied him. He was further startled by the crowd of journalists who showed up, especially since he had done nothing to arrange the gathering.

Before the glare of TV lights and the gallery's one microphone, Mfume promised that there would be no more Democrats-only meetings and that there would be no more overlap and confusion between the Congressional Black Caucus and the Democratic Congressional Black Caucus—not that such a thing existed anyway. Meetings would no longer be adjourned into "Democrats only" conferences and the Democrats could no longer use CBC facilities without paying. The Black Caucus would again become bipartisan. "Can the Congressional Black Caucus accommodate diversity and plurality?" Mfume concluded. "It must. And as long as I am chairman, it will." A reporter asked Mfume if the CBC had agreed to reverse itself because it feared losing money at the CBC Foundation dinner. He quickly brushed her suggestion aside.

My remarks were simple. "All I am asking is for a chance to have my views heard," I said.

After the press conference, Bill Clay's office called and asked my staff to notify him when I would or would not be attending meetings of the Black Caucus. He wanted to arrange his schedule so he could avoid me. We ignored this request. Beyond that, nothing was ever said. I was admitted—if not welcomed back—without further delay. In retrospect, it was an astute performance by Chairman Mfume. He was determined to make the Congressional Black Caucus a far stronger and more influential body than it had previously been.

The African American community has grown best when we have had a variety of voices. We had the H. Rap Browns, the Stokely Carmichaels, the Black Panthers, the Nation of Islam, but we also had voices of moderation—the NAACP, the Urban League, the A. Philip Randolphs, the Roy Wilkinses, and even Dr. Martin Luther King. From the day Martin Luther King was shot until the nomination of Clarence Thomas, the country never heard one black leader criticize another black leader for offering a different approach to social issues. This is suicidal. It opens us to the charge that all blacks think alike. By ostracizing people who express different ideas and branding them as "Uncle Toms," the black leadership creates a uniformity that makes us very vulnerable. It is an echo chamber that is void of ideas. There is no positive movement and very few tangible results.

By accepting me back, the Black Caucus renewed its bipartisan nature. When the political winds shifted and the Republicans gained control of both the House and Senate in 1994, black Republicans became important again. In fact, for a couple of meetings, I do not think that they started until I arrived (only a joke). At my encouragement, the caucus system itself was also revised so that taxpayers would no longer have to support the Black Caucus's annual budget of two hundred thousand dollars. Yet even as the Republicans have seized the agenda, the voices of the black members have remained spirited and relevant.

PART TWO

THE BIG ISSUES

FOURTEEN

Louis Farrakhan and the Million Man March

I T WAS DURING the summer of 1973 that I had my first encounter with the Nation of Islam. I had a summer job at Scovill Manufacturing Company in Waterbury. I mixed with grown men of different races and nationalities.

One black man named Willie befriended me. We used to eat lunch together. Willie would talk about what was going on in the factory and the country. I found him surprisingly well versed for someone who had failed to go much beyond the tenth grade.

After a while, however, I realized that any discussion usually turned into an issue of black versus white people. That in itself didn't bother me. But his arguments inevitably became resentful— although he always spoke in a mild and pleasant way.

I worked as a crane operator that summer. It was one of the better jobs—challenging and paying a good salary. Willie was quick to point out that I had the job because I was a local basketball star and because I went to Yale.

As the days went by, his resentment toward white people grew more obvious. It got to the point of hatred. He started dropping terms like "white devil" in reference to white people. I reacted negatively—which he didn't fail to notice. I knew I had to be careful around him.

Willie began bringing in books about the Black Muslims, trying to recruit me as a member. He told me the Muslims had changed his life. He said that many people who had been in jail for years had had their lives changed permanently by Elijah Muhammad.

I had already learned a lot about the Black Muslims from television and newspapers. My parents were always quick to dismiss the white man—devil belief. During my freshman year at Yale I read *The Autobiography of Malcolm X.* It was notable that before his murder Malcolm saw that the true message of Islam was one of love, not hatred, for anyone.

There was no question in my mind that the Nation of Islam filled a void in the lives of many black men. Often, the worst kid on the block would suddenly turn into one of the best behaved and most disciplined. In many ways, the Nation of Islam fulfilled the role of their absent fathers. It gave members a new name that replaced the name given by their slave owners. It provided an explanation—however fanciful—of the history of race relations and the black man's past. The experience often had concrete results.

But all this was not done without a large dose of hatred. This hatred was directed at both the white man and the Jewish people. Malcolm X had tried to distance himself from this hatred shortly before his murder, but most others hadn't.

For all these reasons, I resisted Willie and his attempts to convert me to the Nation of Islam. He was quite dismayed at this rejection. It probably shook his own faith a little—or perhaps he just classified me among the Jews and white devils. But I'm glad it happened. It prepared me for things to come.

After the 1992 elections, Kweisi Mfume, chairman of the Congressional Black Caucus, persuaded the caucus to strengthen itself by branching out and involving itself with other black-oriented organizations such as the Urban League, the NAACP, and the controversial Nation of Islam. (Mfume left Congress in 1996 to become executive director of the NAACP.)

In his quest for such coalitions, however, he embarked upon what he described as a "sacred covenant" with the Nation of

Islam. This set off alarm bells throughout the press and among prominent Jewish groups. It also proved to be a particularly inopportune time to cozy up to the Black Muslims.

On November 29, 1993, not long after the covenant had been arranged, Khalid Muhammad, one of the Nation of Islam's top ministers and a spokesman for its leader, Louis Farrakhan, made an extremely inflammatory speech at New Jersey's Kean College. At first the speech attracted little notice, but once it was publicized the following January, it fueled a public firestorm.

Muhammad spared no one—Catholics, whites, gays, Jews. He called the pope a "no-good cracker" and added: "Somebody needs to raise that dress up and see what's really under there." He urged black South Africans to kill any whites who refused to flee that nation within twenty-four hours. "We kill the women, we kill the children, we kill the babies. We kill the blind, we kill the crippled, we kill 'em all. We kill the faggot, we kill the lesbian, we kill 'em all," he said.

But it was Muhammad's anti-Semitic rant that produced the most backlash against him. He called Jews "bloodsuckers of the black nation and the black community" and warned blacks about the supposed dangers of "the hook-nosed, bagel-eatin', lox-eatin', impostor-perpetrating-a-fraud, Johnny-come-lately, just-crawled-out-of-the-caves-and-hills-of-Europe, wannabe Jew."

Members of Congress as well as commentators and editorial pages across the country denounced these inflammatory comments. The Black Caucus was having a very tough time wrestling with Khalid Muhammad's incendiary racial and religious slurs. Indeed, the question of the CBC's newfound coziness with the Nation of Islam itself began to furrow more than a few brows.

Meanwhile, the NAACP was enduring its own era of controversy under the leadership of its executive director, Ben Chavis. During his brief tenure at the helm, Chavis tried to build an organization that would elevate the NAACP into *the* top organization representing black Americans with him as the chief spokesman. With the Nation of Islam under fire, it was easier for Mfume and other members of the caucus to participate in events sponsored by the NAACP.

Well before Khalid Muhammad's outbursts, the Black Caucus scheduled a dinner at which Louis Farrakhan would be a featured guest. A number of caucus members wondered why such an event was being arranged. I personally declined the invitation, as did several others.

"Mel, are you going to this Louis Farrakhan dinner?" I asked Mel Reynolds at the time.

"Are you kidding? Are you crazy?" he replied.

"Well, I'm not going either," I said. "I was just wondering if you were." He looked at me in disbelief. Reynolds was an active supporter of Jewish causes in his district. For that reason alone, he would be extremely wary about attending an event that saluted Minister Farrakhan.

We received a brief memo from Representative Mfume about the dinner. It was not a regularly scheduled CBC event, but a separate meeting that had been put together by a few of the members, notably Rep. John Conyers. Mfume reminded us of Farrakhan's words on boosting self-esteem and pride among black men. To my growing amazement, I sensed a tremendous amount of support for the Nation of Islam within the caucus.

I must admit, I still admire some of the work the Nation has done in making black American males more responsible and instilling in them a sense of self-respect. Because of the Nation's tendency toward exploiting and inflaming racial tensions, however, I distanced myself and desired no contact with them whatsoever. When I learned of Khalid Muhammad's racial and religious venom, I immediately took to the House floor to criticize his comments.

Soon after, the U.S. Senate took up a resolution denouncing Muhammad's remarks. It became clear that a similar vote would probably take place in the House. With a great deal of tension, the Black Caucus met to discuss the issue.

Mfume began the meeting by noting that he had told his press secretary to issue a statement denouncing the terms that Khalid Muhammad had used.

Major Owens interrupted him. "Why do we have this covenant in the first place?" he asked. "Is this covenant with the Congressional Black Caucus or is it a covenant that you and Minister Farrakhan have with the caucus? I don't remember ever voting on this matter. For us to look as if we are in favor of this situation is not appropriate."

"I don't remember voting for this covenant either," noted Earl Hilliard.

John Lewis spoke along similar lines. He made it abundantly clear that he did not want to be associated with the Nation of Islam. He thought that its leaders' comments espoused hatred and that we, as a caucus, should take a formal position rejecting such remarks.

Then Carrie Meek chimed in. She said she had heard that a Jewish group had filed a friend-of-the-court brief in the racial gerrymandering case involving Corrine Brown's Florida district. The tone of the meeting went immediately downhill. Instead of discussing the Nation of Islam, members began expressing indignation that a Jewish group would launch a frontal attack on the electoral base of any CBC member. If this were the case, the arguments suggested, why should the caucus be concerning itself about any anti-Semitic attacks?

Charles Rangel expressed the dilemma. "Many of us have members of the Nation of Islam in our districts," he said. "But we have to realize that we also receive a tremendous amount of support from the Jewish community."

The only agreement was that something had to be done. Finally, I spoke up. I said I shared the feelings of Representatives Owens, Lewis, and Rangel that we should condemn Muhammad's comments and renew our effort to rebuild the once-warm relationship between American blacks and Jews. I acknowledged the long, intertwining history of blacks and Jews in our mutual struggle for civil rights and saluted the major contribution that Jews have played in that fight. I pointed out that I did not have a large Jewish population in my district but still had many Jewish supporters—as did other members who had spoken previously.

"Well, you're just supporting them because they give you a lot of money," Rep. Harold Ford interrupted.

"I don't think that's necessarily the case," I responded. "If there were a large number of Jewish individuals on my contributors' list, I would not be ashamed of that. But the fact is there aren't many."

Rep. Earl Hilliard spoke up. "I've been telling the press one thing," he said, "but quite frankly I must admit I agree with Mr.

Muhammad in some respects. Some of the things he says are absolutely true." I saw a faint smile emerge on Rep. Maxine Waters's face.

"I don't see why we should denounce Mr. Muhammad," Cynthia McKinney chimed in. "They [the Jewish people] are engaging in retaliatory acts toward us."

Once again, John Lewis and others disagreed and stated their feelings very clearly. Mfume said he had worked out what he thought was an agreement with Minister Farrakhan. He asked Amelia Parker to get Farrakhan on the phone and stepped away to confer for a few minutes. At that moment, it could not have been more clear just how close a relationship there was between Mfume and Farrakhan. When he returned, he announced that the Nation of Islam would release a statement that Farrakhan denounced the language that Khalid Muhammad had used. Mfume believed that this would resolve things. Most of those in the caucus meeting looked relieved that they would not have to vote on the matter.

The following day, however, it became clear that Minister Farrakhan had not truly separated himself from Khalid Muhammad's remarks. "While I stand by the truths that he spoke," Farrakhan told reporters gathered in a packed Washington, D.C., hotel ballroom on February 3, 1994, "I must condemn in the strongest terms the manner in which those truths were represented." He also demoted Muhammad but allowed him to remain within the group.

This halfhearted disclaimer was unsatisfactory to many members of Congress. The House of Representatives renewed the proposal to denounce both Muhammad and his message. During the hour-long debate on the House floor, an inordinate number of Democratic members argued that Congress should avoid this step. Such a denunciation, they said, was beyond the House's scope and jeopardized freedom of speech. One of those leading this debate was Don Edwards of California, then chairman of the Judiciary Committee's Subcommittee on the Constitution.

On the Senate side, the vote for denunciation had been nearly unanimous. On the House side, there were many nays and many more abstentions. Among them were many members of the Black Caucus, including Mfume. I fear that the NAACP under Mr.

Mfume's leadership may develop a close relationship with the Nation of Islam. This would be to the detriment of the NAACP.

In the early summer of 1995, I heard the first rumors of Minister Louis Farrakhan's proposal for a Million Man March on Washington. I was late for a meeting of the Black Caucus. When I walked in the door, all eyes seemed to focus on me for a moment. The member who was speaking was saying something about a march. He quickly closed and the agenda moved on to something else. I didn't give it much thought at the time.

A few weeks later, I was on national television discussing affirmative action. One of the other guests was Representative Mfume. In the middle of the discussion, he suddenly asked me if I was going to the Million Man March. I replied honestly that I knew very little about it, but I decided I'd better find out.

Once I heard the march was being headed by Louis Farrakhan and Ben Chavis, I began to have my doubts. Farrakhan was attempting to be perceived as a national leader. Chavis had been kicked out of the NAACP because he had used NAACP funds to pay off a former employee who was threatening a sexual harassment suit. He was definitely looking for a new home.

With these two gentlemen leading the parade, my decision was an easy one. There was no way I would support the march. The only question was how much I would make my objections known.

Meanwhile, the other CBC members began lining up behind Farrakhan and Chavis. Some probably had personal reservations and others may have acted out of fear, but the momentum was hard to resist. As Jesse Jackson later commented off-camera during an appearance on *Meet the Press*, "What would it look like if a million black men showed up and I wasn't there?"

Soon after, I received a ballot from the Black Caucus on whether we should endorse the march. I assumed I would be the only one opposed. Since I did not want to call attention to my position, I simply failed to respond. It did not seem to me the event would be attended by large numbers of people.

Soon reporters began asking for my opinion. In September, a black reporter from ABC's *Nightline* tried to buttonhole me while

I was waiting to meet my wife at Washington National Airport. She asked me if I had any problems with Louis Farrakhan leading the march. Before I had a chance to respond, however, my wife rushed up and kissed me and the interview ended. "I think this Million Man March may turn into a real event," I confided to Donna as we headed toward the car.

I was still hesitant to get out front on the issue. Yet the closer we got to the date, the more people began supporting it. In Connecticut, the legislature's black and Hispanic caucus endorsed the event. The Hartford school board actually voted to cancel school on the day of the march to allow students and teachers to attend. (The city council later modified this decision and allowed only excused absences for people who attended.)

It saddened me that people were comparing this event to Dr. King's memorable March on Washington in 1963. That had been a march of inclusion. Everyone was encouraged to come. Farrakhan, on the other hand, essentially forbade white men and black or white women to attend. The spirit was one of exclusion—one that, it seemed to me, black people ought to be rejecting out of hand.

By the Tuesday prior to the march, I literally could not walk from my office to the House chambers without encountering reporters who wanted to ask me about the event. I decided to consult my number one adviser, my wife. I called Donna and asked if she thought I should come out against the march.

"You seem to want to do it already," she said.

"No, I'm asking for advice."

"I would never encourage you to pick a fight."

"I'm not going to try to pick a fight. But I do feel I have to make people aware of my views. I'm going to be all alone on this."

I could tell from her voice she was not thrilled, but she assured me I would do well. We have both always believed that God never gives you more than you can handle. Deciding to face the music, I scheduled a press conference in the Capitol gallery.

A few days before the march, I made the following statement:

I will not be attending nor will I support the Million Man March sponsored by the Nation of Islam and its leader, Louis Farrakhan.

All people in this country of ours can protest, pray, and express themselves. If, however, the Ku Klux Klan were going to march to manifest the concerns of white males, it would represent a sad day for the nation. African Americans would be very concerned, if not outraged.

The Ku Klux Klan expresses hatred for blacks, Jews, and Catholics. The Nation of Islam expresses hatred for whites, Jews, and Catholics. Both organizations should be despised for these warped beliefs. They hide behind a veiled shield of doing what's good for their race while increasing the racial divide via their hatred of others. To give Minister Farrakhan and his organization more prominence will be one of the worst things to happen to race relations in this country.

It does not surprise me that the Congressional Black Caucus is supporting this march. For many members of Congress, race baiting has been a practice. For example, they too believe or have espoused the following: (1) White people are too racist to support a black person; (2) blacks are victims; (3) blacks who disagree with this view are Uncle Toms.

On the other hand, I commend the leadership of the NAACP, the National Urban League, and the Black Baptist Ministers for simply saying that they will not go or support the Nation of Islam's effort.

A difference of opinion is not unique for African Americans. It can be healthy. But anyone who would profess racism and hatred should not have a legitimate place in the dialogue on how we cure our nation's ills. . . .

African Americans had choices in the fifties and sixties with regard to black leaders. On one hand you had H. Rap Brown ("Burn Baby Burn"), Stokely Carmichael, Malcolm X (of the Nation of Islam), and the Black Panthers. On the other, you had leaders such as Roy Wilkins, Whitney Young, Congressman Adam Clayton Powell, and A. Philip Randolph. And, last but not least, there was Dr. Martin Luther King.

Even back then, a vast majority of blacks said "no" to the Nation of Islam and their separatist ways. They said "yes" to the messengers of integration and assimilation.

No, the dream of Dr. King has not yet been realized. We are not living in a color-blind society. But that does not mean we should not continue to strive for this goal.

The first question from the press was "Can't you separate the message from the messenger?"

My answer was "No. If Louis Farrakhan, Ben Chavis, and the people leading the march say you can't separate the message from the messenger, how can I?"

After this statement, I was asked to appear on *Meet the Press, Larry King Live,* and a number of other radio and TV news programs. When we arrived at *Meet the Press,* we were informed that we would do a full hour instead of a twenty-minute segment because Farrakhan had called at the last minute to cancel his appearance. At *Larry King Live,* Farrakhan did appear, along with surprise guest Jesse Jackson. Larry King interviewed Farrakhan first, then he had me on as part of a four-person panel. We all sounded our views with King acting as referee. "This sounds like *Crossfire,*" King said at one point during the heated exchange.

The day after the march, I appeared on the *Imus in the Morning* radio show. In the spirit of the show, I said, "I think Minister Farrakhan should receive an Oscar for an outstanding performance in the category of two-hour documentary." His strange, long-winded speech in which he explored such topics as numerology and the Masons obviously puzzled much of his audience. Thousands and thousands of marchers headed for the exits as Farrakhan droned on. Trying to cut the hate out of his performance, Farrakhan was left without much to say.

I was gratified that President Bill Clinton also worked up the nerve to speak out against the march. I was even happier to see Colin Powell join me in criticizing Farrakhan. Eventually, Rep. John Lewis, activist Angela Davis, and Civil Rights Commissioner Mary Berry all joined me in their nonsupport of the march. I felt a lot less lonely.

You don't have to look very far back in history to find other characters who talked about one people being better than another. No one would dispute the Nation of Islam's call for men to take better care of their wives and children. No one would disagree that those who have abused the family should seek atonement. No one would argue that African Americans as a people should work harder to improve the condition of their families, their community, their country.

But the Nation of Islam is seeking something much different than that. They want African Americans to be exempt from taxation. They would like American blacks to be given their own territory—just as Native Americans were given Indian reservations and blacks in South Africa were given "homelands." They want the United States government to pay massive reparations. In other words, they want a separate black nation. That is a vision shared only by those few white supremacy extremists who are talking of forming a separate white nation in the American Northwest. In either case, it's not going to happen nor should it happen. We are one nation.

After my appearances in opposition to the march, I received the following letter from a woman in Texas:

Dear Congressman Franks:

Thank you for taking the position you did regarding the March on Washington October 16. I was stunned that so many people, black and white, could just brush off the hate-mongering rhetoric of Farrakhan. That racist, divisive message has always been his point of view and I'm just horrified that more people couldn't rebuke him—as you and some others did. It is for this reason that I want to commend you and thank you for reinforcing my belief that principles cannot be abandoned for political expediency.

I do wish you every success and hope that your message got across to the American public and to Black Americans in particular. Reason must prevail—and you came across as a very strong, reasonable, and principled guy.

Good luck in your future ambitions—this country needs more Gary Franks.

I don't know whether she is black or white. But her message is all the reassurance I need.

In spite of our different racial or ethnic origins, we are one nation. The reason we are still able to live together under a magnificent, 208-year-old Constitution is precisely because it is a document designed to help people of different opinions, different backgrounds, and different desires live together in reasonable harmony. The Southern slave owners who wanted their own separate nation were proved wrong—even though it took a great Civil War to carry the point. The same claim of separatism should be received no differently just because an African American like Louis Farrakhan is making it. Together, we must all work toward achieving the promised land of a color-blind society.

FIFTEEN

Affirmative Action

ONE OF THE most difficult issues I have had to deal with in Congress has been affirmative action. As an African American, I am naturally concerned with racial discrimination and all its implications. But I am also concerned about choosing unfair methods of redress that will only heighten racial animosities and cast a shadow of doubt on the legitimate accomplishments of African Americans.

Let me state my position clearly. I am in favor of affirmative action. I am the product of affirmative action. I probably never would have gone to Yale if the university had not begun its outreach program in the 1970s. I directed affirmative action programs during my years in private industry. As I often tell people, my seat in Congress was my first non—affirmative action job.

But I do not endorse all forms of affirmative action. Some broaden the channels of search and lead to the selection of more qualified people. But others represent noxious "counting by numbers" and lead to the selection of less qualified or unqualified people simply because of their gender or race. I approve of the former. I oppose the latter.

The affirmative action efforts I endorse are: (1) outreach programs to new pools of minority and women applicants; (2) enforcement of nondiscrimination laws; and (3) flexible goals and timetables that put government, industry, and educational institutions on notice for meeting their responsibilities.

Those that I do not approve of are: (1) quotas, (2) set-asides, (3) "race norming" of tests, (4) race-based election districts, and (5) anything else that gives minorities or women preferential treatment and amounts to reverse discrimination. Set-asides, quotas, race norming, quotas for the death penalty, and racial gerrymandering are all blood relatives. All are attempts to put a thumb on the scale of justice to arrive at a predetermined result. I have fought them in every shape and size in Congress. In every instance, I have won—and as a result, I believe, the American people have won as well.

Both quotas and race norming were outlawed in the Civil Rights Act of 1991. That bill was approved by 75 percent of the House and 90 percent of the Senate. Racial redistricting has been knocked down by the U.S. Supreme Court. Quotas for the death penalty were kept out of the 1994 crime bill by a majority of Congress. Race- and gender-based set-asides in the awarding of federal contracts, however, is still the law. In 1995, I introduced the Franks amendment, which would outlaw the practice. This effort was rejected by Congress, however, and the issue remains alive.

On the other hand, the outreach programs, enforcement of nondiscrimination, and flexible goals and timetables that I support were all endorsed in the 1991 Civil Rights Act.

Thus, my position is in tune with that of the majority of Americans. Even so, I have been severely criticized in some quarters, particularly by members of the Black Caucus and other African American leaders, who say I am betraying my race. They call me—and anyone who does not accept their opinions—an Uncle Tom.

I am just as concerned as anyone else about the advancement of African Americans. But that does not mean I must march in lockstep with the national black leadership. I believe African Americans must speak with many voices and try different routes to the same goal. We must challenge each other and come up with new ideas. That the majority of blacks and Hispanics in my district regularly give me their votes tells me that there is a lot of support for my positions.

*   *   *

My decision to take on race- and gender-based set-asides began on a Tuesday morning in July 1995, while I was flying back to Washington for a session of the House of Representatives. The Supreme Court had just handed down a decision on the *Adarand* case, in which it ruled that minority set-asides in awarding federal contracts should be more closely scrutinized. The decision reversed a lower court decision that had allowed a person with a higher bid to receive a federal contract over a person with a lower bid simply because the person was a minority. It was clear that the Court was concerned that set-asides were coming very near to being quotas, which had been rejected by Congress in 1991. If that were true in the area of federal contracts, I wondered, why shouldn't it apply to other cases as well?

Wherever race- and gender-based set-asides have been tried, they have been a failure. Look at the program relating to federal contracts. Though the stated goal has been to give 10 to 15 percent of all contracts to companies owned by minorities, the level has never exceeded 4 percent. Yet even this small accomplishment has produced a great deal of animosity among white men, who believe that minorities and women are receiving an undeserved benefit at their expense.

Or take another example: quotas applied to the death penalty. One of the favorite projects of the 103d Congress (the last one controlled by the Democrats) was the Racial Justice Act, which would have allowed condemned murderers to challenge their death sentences on the grounds that disproportionate numbers of blacks are on death row.

In the first place, there is no proof that black murderers are being executed more frequently than white murderers. Nearly half the people on death row are African Americans, but—I am embarrassed to admit this—nearly half the murders in the United States are committed by African Americans. What the studies do tend to show is that a jury is often less likely to impose the death penalty if the *victim* is black. But this could be an argument for *more* executions. Black lives would be more protected if the death sentence were handed out more frequently in cases where blacks are the victim. Yet the Racial Justice Act assured that few people

would ever be executed because there would never be any agreement about what the "quotas" should be based on. (Some
Democrats even suggested that African Americans should make
up only 13 percent of the prisoners on death row because we are
only 13 percent of the general population, regardless of how
many murders are committed.)

Think of the resentments this would create. As I argued on
the floor of the House, "What do we tell Mrs. Jones, whose
daughter has just been murdered? Do we say, 'I'm sorry, Mrs.
Jones, if she had been murdered by a white man, we would be
able to execute him. But because she was murdered by a black
man, we can't, because too many blacks are getting the death
penalty.' How is that going to make her feel about black people? I
think she will seek out the nearest chapter of the Ku Klux Klan."

Quotas and set-asides do not produce fairness or justice. Nor
should minorities and women feel they are gaining anything
when they are the beneficiaries. As a father, I would be embarrassed to have anyone tell me that my children, Azia, Jessica, and
Gary Jr., need special assistance to compete with white children.
That would be telling them they are inferior. I want my children
and all children to be given an equal opportunity, nothing more
and nothing less.

I do not mean to minimize in any way the incredible discrimination that my African American brothers and sisters have experienced in this country. Anyone my age or older remembers vividly
the sight of George Wallace standing in the doorway at the University of Alabama and proclaiming, "Segregation now! Segregation
tomorrow! Segregation forever!" We can remember Lester Maddox
chasing blacks out of his restaurant in Georgia. No black person my
age can forget the civil rights battles or the simple opportunities
that were denied to every one of us. I thank God for the coura-
geous men and women who gave so much—even their lives—to
give us the freedoms and opportunities that we have today.

But that is no reason to turn around and practice discrimination in reverse. Two wrongs don't make a right. We should be
proud of our race, but we should not use race to explain all the
ills of our society. I don't want my children inheriting a world in
which racial counting-by-numbers is everyone's preoccupation.

The civil rights bills of 1964 and 1991 were both designed to eliminate artificial barriers and give everyone the same place at the starting line. Now we must all recognize that the hunt for jobs and careers is not an entirely neutral contest. There are always networks of relatives and friends that give some people the inside track. The sons and daughters of Ivy League graduates are likely to go to Ivy League schools themselves. Many trade unions are called "father-and-son" organizations because they pass down jobs within families and neighborhoods. I have absolutely no objection to having government and private institutions go outside these networks and try to replace them with something more fair and open to all. That is what I did for many years in private industry.

Affirmative action started off in the right direction. As a youngster, I was actually present in 1966 when Lyndon Johnson gave his famous speech on affirmative action at Howard University. I was attending my brother Richard's graduation. Granted, I was too young to understand the intricacies of the speech, but I grasped later that it meant blacks were going to get an equal place at the starting line.

The idea began to take a wrong turn, however, when Parren Mitchell, a congressman of the late 1970s, and others began promoting the idea that blacks and other minorities should receive preferential treatment, even precise numerical set-asides in federal contracts and other areas. The emphasis switched from equal opportunity to unequal opportunity.

In 1978, the Supreme Court's *Bakke* decision prohibited the use of set-asides for admissions to colleges or universities. No one should receive a benefit merely because of his or her skin color. That seemed to settle the matter for good.

But then another practice arose: race norming. On college admissions tests and other competitive exams, blacks and other minorities were given bonus points in order to bring their scores more in line with those of white applicants. What does this say to a black person trying to compete? What does it say to a white or Asian person who sees his or her score surpassed by someone with an unfair advantage? There are some questions about the fairness and objectivity of certain written tests, but that does not mean we need race-based compensation. We should strive to come up with fair tests, not rig the tests at the outset. Race norming was outlawed in the 1991 civil rights bill—a bill that I believe returned us to the original ideals of the 1964 Civil Rights Act.

Make no mistake, I do not believe our society is color-blind. I see discrimination all around me. For example, taxi drivers are notorious for refusing to pick up black fares. They say they are afraid to drive into black neighborhoods for fear of crime, or that they won't be able to get a return fare. Or how about the habit many restaurants have of seating blacks near the kitchen or in the worst locations? If asked to explain, the owner will say, "I have my junior waitresses handling those tables because blacks are not good tippers." Taxi drivers and restaurant owners should not be allowed to get away with these forms of discrimination.

I am a product of affirmative action. Yale recruited aggressively in the cities in the 1960s and 1970s. My credentials were good and my athletic record a plus, but it was still unusual for a person coming out of a small Catholic school in Waterbury to go to Yale. Recruitment had previously focused on prestigious private academies and the affluent suburbs.

But that did not mean Yale lowered its standards. I performed well at Yale and fulfilled their expectations of me. Affirmative action simply meant making a better effort to find people who were qualified. Since I have spoken out against set-asides, the Yale admissions office has been asked by a number of reporters whether blacks have been admitted to Yale under different criteria in recent decades. Whether this relates to my growing profile on the issue of affirmative action, I don't know. In any case, the answer is always the same—"No."

My seat in Congress is obviously not the result of affirmative action. No one comes up to me on the floor of Congress and suggests I'm probably here only because I'm black.

It was heartwarming to me to see Colin Powell taking the same approach during his brief flirtation with the presidency. People talked of him more in terms of a general running for president than a black running for president. Polls showed that his race made very little difference.

Justice Clarence Thomas is another person who would

quickly concede he has benefited from the effort to cast a wider net. As I am, he is the product of urban Catholic schools, which were long overlooked as a route of upward mobility for bright children of working-class backgrounds. But once given the opportunity, he proved himself. What Justice Thomas is attempting to achieve on the Supreme Court is the goal of Martin Luther King—a color-blind society. I admire this immensely and hope that more African Americans will come to appreciate the heroic nature of Justice Thomas's work.

After the passage of the 1991 Civil Rights Act and the Supreme Court decision against racial gerrymandering, you would think we had quotas and reverse discrimination licked. But they keep rearing their ugly head, this time in the form of race- and gender-based set-asides. After the *Adarand* decision, it became clear that Congress would have to deal with the problem again.

In July 1995, I proposed the Franks amendment, which would be a rider to every appropriations bill, forbidding race- and gender-based set-asides. The Republican leadership immediately embraced the idea and we proposed an omnibus resolution that would apply to all appropriations bills. But a number of black organizations—including the Black Caucus—immediately began attacking me.

In August, Jesse Jackson led a march and quasi-sit-in at my offices in Waterbury, demanding to see me. His group sang and chanted protests outside my door. In fact, it was not a very large crowd. When Jackson followed up with a rally at a local church, not one local minister participated. Most of the speakers came from outside my district and outside the state. Jackson has tried three times to rally black voters in my district against me and has failed miserably each time.

Instead of trying to pass laws that bend society out of shape, I concentrate on serving my constituents. African Americans who know me best have always supported me in elections. They know I employ more black staff members and interns than any other congressman in New England. They know I give thousands of dollars in scholarship money to African Americans. They know I have worked with large corporations to get them to fund worthy causes in the black community. They know I have pushed to have black contractors involved in redevelopment projects in down-town Waterbury. The list goes on. Democrats often say, "Let's get more blacks and Hispanics registered in Gary Franks's district so we can beat him." Then someone will whisper, "Don't you know Gary Franks carries those votes?"

A few weeks after my speech, Congressman Ron Dellums confronted me on the floor of the House and started shouting insults in my face. A few of my fellow Republicans said they thought he was going to slug me. It crossed my mind, too, but I was determined that if anybody was going to hit anybody, he was going to hit me first. I was determined not to lose my cool.

I listened for awhile and then turned my back to Dellums. He demanded I turn around and address him. So I did. I calmly but forcefully explained my position to him, talking fast enough so as not to give him any chance to interrupt.

I stressed to him that blacks had grown the most during the civil rights era of the 1950s and 1960s. During that time we had a number of voices, a number of viewpoints, on how to achieve our mutual goal. We tried different routes, but we never questioned the integrity of each other's motives. The diversity of opinion had helped us grow. To have all blacks saying the same thing is neither healthy nor conducive to new ideas.

When I had finished, Dellums and I embraced, repeatedly patting each other on the back. Though we disagreed, we were able to appreciate and respect each other's positions. We both took our seats, knowing we had reached a point of mutual respect, even if we weren't in accord.

After that, it was the Democratic leadership that vowed to stand in the way of the Franks amendment. "Gary, you have every right to ask for a vote," Minority Leader Dick Gephardt told me, "but I guarantee that we'll load it with so many amendments that Congress will be immobilized for weeks." He promised to delay our summer recess if my bill ever reached the House floor.

To my surprise and disappointment, the strategy succeeded. The Franks amendment never reached the floor of the House. The CBC celebrated this as their greatest legislative victory of 1995. In a way, I must agree with them. Yet I suspect the victory will be short-lived. In the summer of 1995, President Clinton gave a speech in which he vowed to "mend affirmative action, not end it." Two months later, he quietly ended set-asides in the awarding of defense contracts. Not one member of the CBC said a word about it. I anticipate that eventually set-asides will be set aside completely.

While I object to reverse discrimination, quotas, and set-asides, I emphatically endorse other forms of affirmative action. We need outreach, enforcement of antidiscrimination laws, plus flexible goals and timetables to overcome the legacy of the past. Ironically, while pursuing quotas and set-asides, we have fallen down in these other areas.

The federal government is doing a terrible job of reaching out to minorities and women as potential government contractors. My office has taken the responsibility of holding seminars to deal with the situation. The job performance and salary increases of cabinet members and department heads should depend upon their success in doing a better job in this area. Right now they lean on set-aside programs as their crutch and alibi. Major government contractors should also be responsible for outreach programs to their subcontractors.

We must also strengthen enforcement of antidiscrimination laws. Today, the Equal Employment Opportunity Commission (EEOC) has a backlog of over one hundred thousand cases. This was never the case when Clarence Thomas ran the agency. I was one of a handful of Republicans to vote to increase funding for the EEOC. It is imperative that every minority and woman should know that we will swiftly and severely punish those who do not treasure the rights of all Americans.

Flexible goals and timetables are also needed to ensure that employers are making a genuine effort to mend the practices of the past. They do not mean that an employer has to hire any particular number of minority individuals or women. The employer is asked to broaden his fields of recruitment, but only the best people are hired. Goals are a way of requiring employers to make that effort. Timetables provide a reference point. If there's no evaluation, you might as well not have a rule. Eliminating goals and timetables without an effective replacement would set us back decades.

Many companies actually prefer quotas because it gives them a bright red line. To them I would say, "You are hurting your company's productivity, increasing racial tensions, and doing a gross disservice to the minority individuals and women whom you employ." They must do better.

At the same time, there is one instance in which I find quotas acceptable. This is where the courts have been forced to step in to remedy a particularly egregious situation. This happened to the city of Waterbury in the 1980s. The city government had resisted all efforts to make it hire more minorities in the police and fire departments. The federal courts stepped in and forced dual-list hiring. For every white hired, the city had to hire a black or Hispanic. Some people were upset by the ruling, but the vast majority of Waterbury citizens recognized that something had to be done.

These situations are rare, however, and are best dealt with by the judiciary. To impose such a program on the entire country through broad legislation would be wrong. At the same time, to overamplify these rare instances and use them to argue that white men everywhere are being treated badly is more than disingenuous. It just ain't so.

Frequently, I am asked how I expect minorities to advance in the economy if we do not practice vigorous hiring quotas to compensate for past discrimination. I always give them the same answer:

1: We need to create an environment of job creation and economic development. In the inner cities, this often means dealing with the problems of safety and crime. Drug trafficking has to be licked. When these areas become safer, more companies will be willing to locate in them.
2: We need a radical approach toward housing and cleaning up old manufacturing sites. We should strive to abolish one of the remnants of the plantation in the twentieth century—public housing. We should also encourage cities to work with other branches of government and the private sector to tear down dormant industrial sites and redevelop them. This may mean easing up on laws about industrial site reclamation,

which are now acting as a huge barrier to redevelopment in urban areas.

3: We must instill a true feeling of hope in our young people. For the indigent who lack role models, there is a special need for attention. As early as possible, we should expose youngsters to real work in summer jobs. We should also create tax incentives that encourage entrepreneurship and economic development in urban areas.

4: We must improve education. A revamping of secondary education along the lines of our very successful college system is an imperative. We cannot keep youngsters trapped in a system that has failed.

5: Last but not least, individual and family responsibilities must be strengthened to enable youngsters to step confidently onto the playing field of life. This means a complete overhaul of "welfare as we know it." We are a generous people, willing to help our neighbors through bad times. But we must also let everyone know that this assistance does not extend for life but must eventually be paid back in some manner.

I have given much thought to these issues and will be making a number of proposals in the following chapters.

PART THREE

A BLUEPRINT
FOR HOPE

SIXTEEN

Careers and Hope

WHEN I was growing up, my brother participated in Junior Achievement. Later, as a corporate manager for Peter Paul Cadbury, I realized the value of this program for young people. It allows eighth graders or high school students to run a real business. With the supervision of managers, Junior Achievement participants actually make or lose money. Students select the officers of their company and each person plays a part. When I heard what my brother was doing in Junior Achievement, it perked my interest.

When I was in grade school, we all had to take a course that seemed to have little to do with schoolwork. For boys it was called "shop," for girls it was "home ec." I hated it. For the life of me, I could not figure out why it was in the school curriculum. Today I understand its value. It was preparing us for family living. I think the schools should teach household finance and parenting as well—not as a stopgap after teenagers have already had their first child but as a program for everyone.

Hopes and dreams typically originate in the family. To see a father or mother, aunt or uncle pursuing a career makes a huge difference. Most middle-class children have role models for many kinds of careers.

For African Americans, these role models are too often limited to celebrities in sports, dancing, singing, acting, and comic roles.

Granted, we may know about a local barber or beautician. We recognize the mortician and the minister. Maybe there are a few schoolteachers on our horizon as well. But for most indigent people in this country, if you ask them about Wall Street, they are likely to respond, "Isn't that near Orange or Willow Street?" This is sad.

Slaves had little hope. I am sure my forefathers dreamed about their lost villages. They remembered loved ones left behind and thought God had touched them with death. If anything kept my forefathers going, it was the dream of regaining their freedom. The old Negro spirituals cried out for it.

I have always been a follower of the old adage, "If you can believe it, you can conceive it." My life is a testament to that and I hope with the help of God and a loving family it can happen for others as well.

When black schoolchildren tell me of their dreams of playing professional basketball, I am often tempted to discourage them and throw water on their dreams. Then I catch myself. Instead, I try to give them a backup plan. I tell them my story. I walk them through a scenario in which they might become a doctor or lawyer or investment banker. I tell them if they are good at these professions they would quickly make as much money as the average basketball player. Moreover, they would be able to pursue this occupation at fifty-six as well as twenty-six. Business and professional people get better with age. Athletes' careers are quickly over—sometimes before they've barely started. Look at what happened to Bo Jackson.

The solution, I think, is to inform the indigent and disenfranchised youngster about career possibilities. Why not develop a series of videotapes that would give young people a feel of what it would be like to be an accountant, chemist, or electrical engineer? The videotapes could be shown to children in the fifth and eighth grades and again when they are seniors in high school. They would go into lengthy detail on what you have to do to prepare for such a profession, what it's like to work in the profession, and what kind of salaries and work environment you can expect. Such videotapes would be part of every school and city library. I believe private industry would pay the entire cost.

Today, one of every three black men between the ages of twenty and twenty-nine is in jail or on probation or parole. At that point, it is almost too late to raise people's sights. We need to stimulate the hopes of indigent youngsters early so they can dream the same dreams as middle-class youngsters.

SEVENTEEN

Summer Jobs

IN THE PAST, most government-sponsored summer job programs have involved employing impoverished youngsters in govern- ment agencies. When I was growing up, those who were fortu- nate—or politically connected—were usually able to land a job with the city parks or recreation programs. Typically, this involved supervising younger children or patrolling the parks for trash. Numerous cousins of mine participated in such programs.

At bottom, these jobs were little more than make-work efforts. Some kids were known to complete their day's work in two hours, while being paid for eight. Others swept the same floor many times a day. Most of these jobs were not really needed, or could have been done with far fewer people.

A much better way to provide summer jobs would be to encourage private companies to employ these youngsters in posi- tions of real responsibility. In many companies where I worked during my business career, I saw children of managers and direc- tors and vice presidents readily given summer employment. Yet for most impoverished children, this advantage does not exist.

My first job was at Waterbury Hospital. I got it because my mother worked there. I did what no one else wanted to do— cleaning the toilets, washing the pots and pans, mopping the floors. On a good day I washed dishes or served food in the hos- pital cafeteria. There was not a lot of skill involved, but there was a paycheck at the end of the week and the job broadened my horizons.

I talked with other employees and ended up learning a lot about the operation of Waterbury Hospital. I saw the hospital operated on a priniciple of teamwork that was similar to sports. People had roles to play. While doing the dishes, I would often say to myself, "What would happen if I did not do the pots and pans tonight? Could I shut down the hospital because they would not be able to prepare the food for the patients the next morning?" Obviously, I did not have that kind of power. But I did see that by doing my job I played an integral role in the smooth running of the hospital.

Why not create a summer job program that would give other youngsters the same opportunity? Currently, almost all the money spent on summer job programs goes through government agencies. Why not use half those dollars to place youngsters in private companies that would expose them to the workings of the economy? This would be the Republican version of the summer jobs program.

Each qualifying youngster could be given a government voucher that would be worth half a week's pay. An individual employed at five dollars an hour for forty hours would receive one hundred dollars each week from the company and another one hundred dollars from the government. The program, of course, should not be used to displace adult full-time workers. But summer vacation is a time when many companies are seeking extra help.

As part of the program, the company would be required to expose youngsters to various parts of their operation. This would put flesh on people's career aspirations. It would allow them to see role models—positive ones. Youngsters would see what real work is like—punching the clock, following orders, getting the job done. Even mail room employees learn by osmosis. The impact would be tremendous. It would create hope and allow people to dream.

No company would be forced to take part in this program. Yet from my experience in the business world, I believe most companies would want to participate. It would allow them to play a more active role in curing the ills of society. They would be performing a valuable social service while helping their bottom line.

As Republicans we cannot spell change "b-u-d-g-e-t c-u-t-s." I believe we must define change by saying, "Since this program hasn't worked, let's try something new."

EIGHTEEN

School Choice

THOUGH WE once boasted one of the best school systems in the world, we have fallen behind due to the archaic way in which we administer our elementary and secondary education.

In many communities, the board of education is the largest employer and the largest item in the city or town budget. Schools are a big business—and heavily unionized as well. Just about all teachers and administrators have union representation. The National Education Association, which represents public school teachers, is now the largest labor union in the country, having surpassed the Teamsters in 1986.

The whole spirit of unions is to get something in addition to what they already have. Granted, an increase in wages is something all working Americans want. But teachers' contracts regularly extend far beyond pay scales to include the number of hours they spend inside the classroom, lunchroom responsibilities, and seniority rules that make it difficult to put the best teacher in the right job. All this hampers the flexibility needed to improve the school systems.

I am not against teachers. As I have already mentioned, three of my sisters and one brother have worked as teachers. However, we have to recognize that constructive change flies directly in the face of the contracts under which most teachers and administrators now work.

Try raising the number of hours a student will be taught and you will run right up against the terms of the teachers' contract. Yet spending more time in class means more opportunity to learn. A number of countries, including Japan and Germany, spend far more classroom hours teaching their youngsters than we do. It would seem the public should cry "foul!" Yet under the current system, parents are helpless to demand changes.

Strangely enough, while our elementary and high school education has fallen behind, our colleges have maintained their best-in-the-world status. People come from all over the globe to attend colleges and universities in the United States of America. Why the difference?

The answer is simple: competition. At the college level, every school would like to have the best students. At the same time, the best students want to go to the best schools. Somehow, the two manage to court and marry each other. We have liberal arts colleges, engineering schools, business schools, technical schools, and so forth. People have a choice and use it to go to a school they like.

The issue of introducing educational choice at the level of high school and even grade school has been batted around now for several years. I find it ironic that people such as the members of the Congressional Black Caucus reflexively oppose school choice, even though it would offer to ordinary people the advantages that they often choose for themselves. President Clinton is against school choice, but he sends his own daughter to a private school. Many members of Congress do the same thing, as do other well-to-do people around the country. The attitude is that what's good for me isn't necessarily good for you.

My parents scraped and saved to send me to Catholic high school. It was a very limited choice, but one that they thought was essential. It made a huge difference in my life. Other kids I knew would have liked to go to Catholic school but their parents couldn't afford it. I think that kind of option should be open to everyone.

People oppose school choice for a number of reasons. They argue that children will choose a school only because it has a good sports program or because they want to be with their friends. But so what? A limited number of people do this at the college level and it doesn't hurt education. People are responsible for their own choices.

Opponents also argue that a choice system that included religious schools would violate the Constitution. But federal aid already goes to religious colleges—the Yeshivas, the Notre Dames, the Texas Christians—and nobody objects.

Perhaps most important, opponents of choice argue that public choice would divide us as a nation. All the smart children will opt for private schools and public schools will be left with the worst students. We would become divided by class and opportunity. Yet this is already happening in the present system. In many urban areas, anyone who can has already abandoned the public schools. What we need is a system that would revitalize public education for the benefit of those who need it most.

The main problem with the public schools is that, even in the sad shape they are in today, they are largely insulated from competition. Year after year, district schools are guaranteed a "customer base," regardless of how badly they perform. Like any monopoly, the school system is soon run for the benefit of its own employees rather than the consumers. Teachers go on piling up vacations and benefits, increasing their free time, and moving out of the classroom and into bloated bureaucracies. As a result, the public schools have ended up looking like 1970s American corporations, with huge bulges in "middle management," rather than the lean, efficient American corporations of the 1990s.

Pay scales are determined solely by the number of years on the job and the number of graduate credits acquired. This is the way the unions want things to be. Performance counts for nothing. The unions prefer to secure benefits for their oldest, most faithful members, while keeping younger, ambitious members from rocking the boat.

In our colleges, on the other hand, teachers who have outstanding track records are sought out by students and other colleges as well. Those teachers make more money and have a better benefits package. Why? Because the colleges feel they deserve it. Pay scales are tied to performance, not mere longevity.

It would be easy enough to evaluate teachers' performance in the public schools. Test a teacher's class in basic skills at the beginning of the year and then test them at the end of the year to see how far they have progressed. The comparison could be the basis of evaluating the teacher.

The best test, however, is how satisfied parents are with their child's education. If parents are able to pull their children out of a particular school because they don't like a teacher, then they have passed their judgment. Parents are the best judges. I know of few parents who are dissatisfied because their children are learning too much in school.

Teachers' unions and their allies in the Democratic Party always argue that "more money" is the only solution to the problem. In a sense, they hold the children hostage. "Give us more money or we will not improve your children's education," they say. In some labor disputes, unionized teachers have refused to write college letters of recommendation for their students as a way of bargaining for better contracts.

Yet "more money" obviously makes little difference. Washington, D.C., spends more than ten thousand dollars per pupil for a system that is falling apart. The problem is that the vast majority of parents still have only one choice—the public school in their district. Unless they make huge sacrifices to send their children to private schools—or move to another district—they have no way of demanding improvements from the system.

Some people argue that, given complete freedom of choice, parents with money would up the ante for tuition at private schools. These schools would then accept children according to what they could pay, rather than their scholarship. Once again, we would be divided into a rigid class system.

My own experience tells me differently. Ivy League schools do not take financial resources into account when they admit a student. They accept people according to scholastic achievement and deal with finances later. This is called "need-blind" admissions. Yale could easily double its tuition and accept only the sons and daughters of the richest families in America. Instead, the school determined long ago that emphasizing scholarship and a diverse student body was the best way to create an outstanding educational environment. Most elementary and secondary schools would do the same. Any school that didn't would quickly earn the reputation as a "rich kids' playground" and lose its appeal.

At the same time, there are some students who, I believe, should not have school choice. These are the children who are disciplinary problems. I think schools should be allowed to expel students who ruin the educational environment for other children. Those children should be assigned to schools that deal only with children who have similar problems, with the understanding that they can rejoin the mainstream if they learn to behave.

When I was at Sacred Heart, Father Blanchfield had the ability to throw out any student at any time for any reason. Only a very tiny percentage of students were ever expelled. But the threat kept other students in line and created an environment in which everyone was able to learn. Why not give all school principals the same authority?

As a last resort, parents should also be allowed the option of "home schooling." If parents believe they can provide a better learning environment than public or private schools, they should be able to make that choice.

The driving force in our current school system is misplaced. Schools have been viewed as a public utility best provided by a government monopoly. In order to maintain this monopoly power, it is necessary to handicap or outlaw the competition.

This is wrong. Competition should be the model. We have a great country because of the competitive nature of our society. Competition brings out the best in all of us. Why not make the competition we have at the collegiate level the model for improving education in our elementary and secondary school systems?

NINETEEN

Family Development Charities

IN 1993, I introduced a bill that would encourage individuals and corporations to give to charities that foster family development by giving them a 100 percent or greater tax write-off for charitable contributions.

The concept of getting the haves to help the have-nots is one that I have espoused for years. When I began my political career, charitable contributions were still quite high. Then came the 1986 tax bill, which reduced the benefits of charitable gifts for tax write-offs. The change made quite a difference.

Prior to introducing my bill, I toured the Boys' and Girls' Clubs in my district. I had fond memories of all these places. Growing up, I frequented the Boys' Club and the YMCA of Waterbury. I grew as a person from my experiences with them. In later years I served on the board of directors of both these organizations.

Unfortunately, in recent years, I discovered, donations have fallen off considerably. The administrators of these organizations attribute the decline directly to the tax bill of 1986. Although I like the lower tax rates of the 1986 reform, I believe the reduction of benefits for charitable deductions is a flaw that should be reconsidered.

Before the development of our current welfare system under President Franklin Roosevelt, much of the work of helping the needy was done by private charities. People were struggling to provide for their families, but they managed to survive. We provided for our poorer Americans without a huge federal bureaucracy. We did not redistribute vast amounts of dollars through tax-funded welfare programs. The haves helped the have-nots without being required.

I firmly believe that if the welfare state had not been created by President Roosevelt, we would have continued to provide for the indigent in a responsible manner. We also would have avoided creating a slavelike environment in which people remain helplessly dependent from generation to generation. Given the choice between having their dollars go to a charity of their choice and having it disappear into the deep, dark hole of the federal government, we know what most people would choose.

My bill would allow dollar-for-dollar tax deductions for any contribution up to $10,000 to any charity that encourages family development. A person making a contribution between $10,000 and $50,000 would get a 120 percent write-off. Contributions between $50,000 and $100,000 would get a 133 percent deduction, and contributions over $150,000 would be worth 150 percent.

Though my bill addresses only individual contributions, I believe corporations should be involved as well. I have personally persuaded several major corporations in my district to make charitable contributions. PRIDE, the Granville Academy, the Hispanic Coalition, and the Waterbury NAACP (despite the state organization's opposition to my candidacy) have all been beneficiaries.

I see little resistance in the corporate hierarchies once people understand the importance of these donations. If we are going to shrink government, private charities and their contributors are going to have to step up to help. Most corporate officials understand and appreciate this. Why not put incentives in place to encourage even more giving by these financial giants?

By strengthening our charities, we can build a nonprofit-based community network of family development institutions that will help to replace the welfare state. We will not only reduce government and relieve the burden on middle-class taxpayers but also improve life for the indigent.

TWENTY

Pleasures versus Evils

W HAT IS THE cheapest form of entertainment known to man or woman? You guessed it—sex. If you were sitting on a plantation during slavery or sitting in a housing project in Harlem today, it would rank as the number one diversion.

Illegal drugs, unfortunately, would be a close second today. In some locales, they may even be number one. Having never used illegal drugs, I don't know. As a child, I did make a lot of model cars and airplanes and may have accidentally sniffed enough glue to qualify. But as far as I know, I have never been "high" in my life, so I can't speak from experience.

Also near the top would be music. People have always entertained themselves by singing and dancing. Together, these three would make up the entire menu of entertainment for people who had very little else in their lives.

Sex and music were among the limited pleasures that my forefathers enjoyed—if they enjoyed anything—since the time they arrived in this land in 1619. None of these practices disturbed the slave owners. In fact, sexual diversion was encouraged because it meant more hands for production. Sex was also a diversion for the slave owners themselves. The many mulatto children who were the products of these encounters are the evidence. These "darkies," who were noticeably less dark than their brethren, formed the first upper class of the slave population.

Often they were allowed to learn to read. The law generally forbade blacks to get any education, but blood proved thicker than water—or the law. This proved to be a breakthrough. Frederick Douglass, who believed his owner was also his father, went on to become an internationally recognized scholar and abolitionist.

Today, with a great deal of idle time on their hands, welfare recipients also have plenty of time for sex. It represents one of the few means to something pleasurable. This is the general attitude in our society. Listen to the radio or watch daytime television and you will hear a lot of loose talk about sex. It often amazes me that the middle class wonders why poor people have so many children.

Drugs, on the other hand, allow a person to escape from reality. This is the mind-set of many disenfranchised youth. After all, their world is not filled with joy or hope, is it?

At one time, running the numbers game—along with pimping and prostitution—was one of the best-paying professions in poor neighborhoods. Now the numbers game has been legalized in order to raise money for the state—perhaps our most regressive form of taxation. Illegal drug dealing has largely replaced numbers running as a career path. It has grown to such a degree that whole corporate entities—known as "gangs"—have been formed to administer the supply and demand. As a result, lives and families have been destroyed.

The pressure that this breakdown of community standards has put on young people has been enormous. Among my own friends in Waterbury was a black family that was one of the most successful in town. The father owned his own construction company. He and his wife sent their daughter to college, where she trained to be an accountant. She got involved in drugs, however, and began stealing from her parents. Finally, she went to a mortgage loan company and impersonated her mother. She took out a twenty-five-thousand-dollar loan on a previously mortgage-free house. When the mother discovered this deception, they had a huge confrontation. The daughter and her boyfriend strangled and stabbed the mother to death. They even had the nerve to go to her funeral as if nothing had happened. Luckily, for society's sake, she was apprehended and convicted. But, oh, what a tragedy! What a waste of a talented, attractive black family. Only a few years later, the father died of a broken heart.

If someone had said to my slave forefathers, "How could your situation be made worse?" they would have argued that nothing could be worse than what they experienced as slaves. Now they might answer differently. The world of crack cocaine and other illegal drugs has produced a slavelike existence that may be worse than anything my forebears experienced. During slavery there was nothing that could warp people's minds to the point where they would turn on their own parents or sacrifice the well-being of their own children. But that is what illegal drugs do today. Physicians say that the desperate desire for crack actually overpowers the maternal instinct and makes a mother abandon her children. And, of course, we read every day of instances where it has made children turn on their parents.

Unfortunately, the problem is getting worse. The fear of contracting the AIDS virus might be thought of as one way to curb drug usage, but there is no evidence that even the threat of getting infected needles has discouraged drug abuse. A seemingly benevolent idea is to have the government give out clean needles to address the problem. Yet I strongly disagree. To me it sounds like giving up altogether: We can't address the problem, so let's just go along with it.

There are far more constructive ways to deal with the situation. Increasing hope in people's lives, along with drug rehabilitation and treatment, are vital. A true war on drugs, such as Presidents Reagan and Bush waged, represents a step in the right direction. The impact that countries such as Colombia and Turkey have on this country with their illegal supplies of cocaine and opium seems comparable to a state of war.

We now have whole neighborhoods of children being victimized by this combat. Are we asleep or just looking the other way? In light of all this, President Clinton's efforts to cut back the work started by former drug czar William Bennett seems incomprehensible. We should take the same attitude toward foreign drug dealers as we took toward Saddam Hussein.

People laugh at former First Lady Nancy Reagan's "Just Say No" program, yet the numbers showed that it did have a positive effect. Moreover, it cost next to nothing. That illegal drug usage has gone back up during the Clinton administration is proof that the retreat of our president has had an adverse impact.

A serious drug strategy could go a long way toward improving race relations in this country. African Americans tell me all the time, "If the United States could put a man on the moon, don't tell me it can't stop drug trafficking in this country." I agree. Illegal immigration falls into the same category. The most powerful country in the world should be able to protect its own borders.

In the eyes of many African Americans, the failure to stop the drug trade shows an irresponsible neglect. The often-talked-about conspiracy theory of race relations is at the root of the problem, as far as many blacks are concerned. "The Man" just wants it to happen. For whites, it reinforces racial stereotypes: "Oh, they're not human, they're just animals." My forefathers heard it and I hear it again today. Stopping the drug trade is one way the government could step up to the plate and solve a problem that disproportionately affects African Americans.

The ironic thing is that illegal drugs never would have been tolerated on a slave plantation. It represented too much of a threat to the slave owner's investment. Only because lower-class African Americans are now regarded as marginal to society does America allow this scourge to continue. It is time to end the twentieth-century slavery of drug addiction.

TWENTY-ONE

Job Creation

I<small>N ORDER TO</small> have a robust economy, we must help employers to
employ employees. This sounds like a tongue twister, but it is
very basic:

1. We need to ease government regulations in many areas.
2. We need a significant reduction in the capital gains tax.
3. We need more extensive tax credits for research and development.
4. We need to balance the federal budget.
5. We should adopt the Urban Entrepreneurs Opportunity Act
   mentioned in chapter 10.
6. We must rebuild.

People producing honest jobs should be helped. People risking
their capital to increase their capacity to provide a service or
product should be helped. Companies willing to take on the challenge of embarking into a new area should also be encouraged.

For decades, thanks to the free enterprise system and hardworking people, we have invented, produced, and dominated new
industries. When I was growing up, if you bought something
made in Japan, people snickered because it was assumed to be
cheap. Now, one would be hard-pressed to find a television, VCR,
toaster, refrigerator, or any appliance that has been manufactured

in the United States. The Japanese have remodeled their economy toward quality manufacturing and now dominate many consumer lines.

Years ago we led the world in consumer products. This gave us a very favorable trade surplus. During the 1980s, our growing trade deficit hurt us badly. We cannot tolerate a one-way trade with the Japanese or anyone else for very long. We must insist on free and open trade. At the same time, if Japanese products are superior, we should not prevent people from buying them. The answer is to untie our own hands so that we can become more productive and profitable.

Government regulations have added to the cost of American products. They have made us less competitive in the international market. Safety regulations are one thing, but when we become so obsessed with minor concerns that we damage the health of our industries, we are hurting ourselves in a different way.

The Republicans of the 104th Congress have tried to instill common sense into our federal regulations. Money spent on exaggerated dangers and alarms is money wasted. In the school systems, for example, millions of dollars have been spent tearing out small amounts of asbestos that pose no threat at all. In fact, removing the asbestos is usually a greater risk than leaving it in place. The same kind of make-work effort on environmental and safety issues takes place in industry every day. We need to be concerned about the environment and safety conditions, but we must recognize that wrongly directed effort in these areas has its own costs.

A capital gains tax cut would allow people producing jobs to keep more of their earnings, which can in turn be used to produce more jobs. A cut in the capital gains tax would make buying and selling stocks more attractive. It would increase investment. This would help small businesses as well as large. One of our nation's greatest success stories is the growth of the small business sector. This sector produces the most job growth and is most sensitive to changes in tax policies. A capital gains tax cut would help small businesses expand their operations.

I am firmly convinced that a cut in the capital gains tax would also be a revenue producer rather than a revenue loser. This is not

a matter of faith. The statistical record proves it. Only the dema-
goguery of a capital gains tax reduction as a "tax cut for the rich"
prevents us from realizing this enormous benefit to our economy.

A significant *increase in research and development* credits would
also stimulate business toward new technological breakthroughs.
This stimulus would affect industry but would also roll back
through the colleges and universities, where science and engineering departments would gear up for the new demand for technical skills.

Many foreign nations work with their private sectors in developing new products. We don't want government directing the private economy. But we do want the government to make it easier
for private firms to achieve technological breakthroughs. Over the
past five decades, government-sponsored research has concentrated on our defense needs. This was necessary in fighting the
Cold War. No one would deny that we make the best tanks,
fighter planes, missiles, submarines, etc. But research must now
shift toward consumer-oriented fields. This is best done by private companies. Corporations are placing too much emphasis on
the next quarter's profits versus the next decade's profits. This
approach will hurt us all.

Finally, we must *balance the federal budget.* Our economy is
never going to reach its potential until we stop mortgaging our
future by draining three hundred billion dollars out of the
economy every year. Balancing the federal budget would leave
every citizen with more money in his or her pocket. It would
bring down interest rates at least 2 percent. That would reduce
the average home buyer's monthly payments from one thousand
dollars to eight hundred dollars on a mortgage of one hundred
thousand dollars. Car loans, business loans, and student loans
would all realize the same savings. Americans would be left free
to pursue their own ambitions, rather than pay off the ever-
mounting burden of government debt. It would be the most positive thing we could do to stimulate our economy.

For some reason, Republicans have been branded as the party
that "lacks compassion." I have been to countless congressional
hearings at which liberal Democrats make no contribution to
shaping new approaches to problems but only sit and call Repub-

licans heartless for trying to replace programs that have obviously failed. Democrats always define compassion as spending other people's money—even if those "other people" are future generations of Americans. For decades, the only solution they could think of was to increase federal outlays. Now we are saddled with a national debt that—if it is not dealt with—may ensure that the next generation of Americans cannot possibly live as prosperously as we do. Who is it now that lacks compassion for these future generations of Americans?

The Urban Entrepreneurs Opportunity Act should be the last piece of the puzzle. It would encourage large corporations to participate in the revitalization of depressed urban and rural areas. *Fortune* 1000 companies would be asked to contribute up to ten million dollars and donate administrative assistance to people willing to start or expand businesses in state or federal enterprise zones.

Many large companies will not now locate in crime-ridden urban areas. Yet I believe they would be willing to make both a financial and personnel commitment under the following conditions:

1. The contribution toward the revolving loan fund would be treated like any other charitable contribution, such as to the United Way or the American Red Cross.
2. The companies would stand a chance of recovering some of the loan money if the businesses are successful. (Loans would be made at slightly higher rates than banks offer.)

There would be the additional advantage that the companies would be developing business ties with growing enterprises. As depressed areas begin to recover, these companies would be in a prime position to take advantage of their improving consumer markets.

Billions of dollars could be derived from such an effort. These dollars would foster a whole generation of budding entrepreneurs and small businesses in depressed neighborhoods. It would eventually go a long way toward lifting the welfare and social services burden that the government now bears. It represents exactly the kind of special assistance our depressed cities and towns could best use.

Rebuilding our economy will mean converting many industries from cold-war defense back to commercial work. For decades, many regions of the country have prospered from defense contracting. Now that need is gone. Although conversion may seem straightforward, in reality many of these industrial sites have become contaminated. The unrealistic environmental laws of the last decade have made it all but impossible to reuse these urban properties. If a site is not 100 percent clean, previous owners can be held liable for future problems. Industries are finding it easier to move to suburban "greenfields" rather than deal with the problems of waste in urban areas.

One of my proudest accomplishments in Congress has been to help the city of Waterbury recycle such an urban industrial site. Waterbury was once known as the "Brass Capital of the World." During World Wars I and II, the Defense Department persuaded Scovill Manufacturing Company to expand its production of munitions. The new buildings—right in the heart of Waterbury— were so militarily oriented that they were built to withstand a bombing attack.

In the late 1970s, the Defense Department scaled down production and Scovill closed the site. Mayor Edward Bergin asked me to help put together a plan whereby the federal government would clear the site and make it available for new development. After going over the documents, we quickly realized that there was a paragraph that took the federal government off the hook in terms of restoring the property to its original condition. As a result, a prime piece of real estate in downtown Waterbury would be left abandoned.

Up until hours before Bill Clinton was sworn in as president, I had been working with the Bush administration to try to find the twenty-million-dollar federal contribution needed to clean up the site. Secretary of Defense Dick Cheney informed me that the only way to appropriate the money would be through legislation. No one expected it to pass. Mayor Bergin was working even harder to get the money from the state government.

Finally, through the efforts of Rep. Joe McDade (R-Penn.), ranking member of the appropriations committee, the House of Representatives approved twenty million dollars to clean the site.

The Senate failed to allocate any money for the project; thus the figure was later reduced to five million dollars in the House and Senate conference committee. The Homart Sears Corporation had agreed to construct the second-largest mall in New England if we would demolish and clean the site. The real key to selling the project was the fact that we had an end user in place.

Projects of this nature should be duplicated all across this country. It was a perfect marriage of entities, with city, state, federal, and private support all playing a part. The project will remove an eyesore from the heart of the community and produce thousands of new jobs. We are making the successful conversion from defense plants to a consumer-related economy.

I want the federal government to play a role in financing such tasks, but not through raising taxes. The effort should be a part of defense conversion and urban redevelopment. The boom years in the industrial Northeast were bought, to a large degree, through military buildup and defense contracting. Now we have to convert to new times. Why not set up a fund for cleaning up downtown sites? We can help rebuild America by literally rebuilding our urban cores.

PART FOUR

REFORMING
WELFARE

TWENTY-TWO

Welfare versus Slavery

THE CURRENT welfare system is really a form of slavery. The common core is dependence. The slave is completely dependent upon his master for food, clothing, housing, and sustenance. He has all forms of choice and freedom taken away from him. The slave does what the master tells him, doesn't ask any questions, and is kept alive.

There's hopelessness in both slavery and welfare. You're trapped, you can't control your destiny, and if you try to escape, good luck.

In slavery, economic calculation overrode the interests of family. Fathers were separated from their wives and children — even mother and child were sold apart. The only rule was that everyone would be housed, clothed, and fed.

The same thing is happening today in the housing projects where children and adults sit around all day watching television. Welfare creates the same kind of minimal existence. People are given just enough to live on in exchange for changing their behavior in very destructive ways. What are the rules they must obey? First, they must have a baby out of wedlock. Second, they must keep the baby's father a secret. Third, they must not allow the father to live with them. There must be no "man in the house." If they do all three of these things, they can collect welfare.

The consequences of this system on the African American community have been devastating. People say the black family never recovered from slavery, but that isn't true. There were tremendous pressures on the black family, that's for certain. Sons, daughters, husbands, and wives were sold to different plantations. And, of course, slave owners confused things even more by forcing themselves on slave women and adding their own progeny to the slave population.

But that didn't mean an end to the black family. Surveys show that in the 1920s, '30s, and '40s, black families formed two-parent households at a rate that equaled and sometimes even surpassed that of their white counterparts. It was only with the welfare system and its perverse incentives that things started to fall apart.

When I was a kid, we still had something called "shotgun weddings." If a boy got a girl pregnant, the two fathers would get together and make an arrangement—which was that the boy and girl would get married. It may not have been an ideal system, but I know some shotgun marriages that have lasted thirty years and more. It was a system that held the family together, and when the family holds together, the community holds together. You don't have a lot of unattached young men running around with no other responsibility in life than to get high and create trouble for other people. You don't have a lot of welfare mothers who are encouraged to stay home and do nothing because if they work they lose their welfare benefits. You don't have a lot of unsupervised children who are being introduced to adult life too early and who are soon breeding the next generation of hopelessness.

Without question, African Americans have had to deal with enormous and unique difficulty since our arrival in 1619. It is an experience to which few others in the United States can relate. During the long journey to America, only the strongest physically and mentally survived. Many perished because they failed to accommodate to the rigors of the ordeal. Those who survived were special beings.

I can only imagine my forefathers in Africa, proud and strong, loving and family-oriented, being forced to come to a foreign land among people speaking a strange tongue, with ways different from their own. They were immediately confronted with a superior technology. Guns and gunpowder outmatched them, allowing the few to control the many. I can only imagine the pain they felt when put in chains and divided from their loved ones.

It must have been difficult for my forefathers to understand why this was happening to them. Yet as days turned to months and month to years, it became obvious that the separation was permanent. We as a people fell deeper and deeper into despair. Hopelessness became the order of the day. God was the only hope—and religion the only common denominator between slave and master.

The one chance slaves had for advancement was to be on their best behavior and to be promoted to the "big house." This gave them a little better food and shelter and got them out of the hot August sun. Yet even then, life must have seemed puzzling. The slaves did all the work but the slave owner in the big house seemed to reap all the rewards. Isolation was the slave master's key strategy. No one in the big house could become too familiar with the slaves—other than for sex. Yet despite the master's best efforts, slaves learned to read and write—skills that were supposed to be reserved for the white man. The church also provided a vehicle that allowed the slaves to congregate.

It is not easy to tell someone who has been dependent to go out and be a free man. After the Emancipation Proclamation, many slaves did not know what to do. They became sharecroppers mainly because it kept them within familiar surroundings. My great-grandfather did just that. He became a tobacco sharecropper. It was a very, very difficult road, but he eventually acquired land and became a relatively successful farmer.

With freedom comes responsibility. African Americans reacted magnificently to their freedom. They built strong local economies and businesses in many communities. At the turn of the century, there were African American banks, insurance companies, and even a few black millionaires. But these people had a strong community behind them. They were supported by millions of black families, working hard to raise their children and hoping for a better life.

The welfare system has now destroyed much of that economic base. People no longer work for a living. They depend on handouts from the government. Young men, freed from the responsibility of supporting their children, become involved in crime and the drug trade. They seek a life of big scores and easy highs. All social responsibility is gone.

The parallels with slavery are sickening. The male only breeds, while the mother is left to care for the child. The system handles all the expenses. People fail to form true families and true communities. Yet no man is an island. We have to work hard to pull the family unit back together if we are going to restore order in the black community.

I am making a very general statement that really only applies to the so-called underclass. There are thousands of blacks who have strong families that love, work, and play together.

But we are never going to make strong families the norm until we change the welfare system. I am hoping that the welfare reform bill, which is still before Congress, will be a big step forward. Since 1991, I have been chairman of the Welfare Reform Task Force for the Republican Party in Congress. We have been offering legislation that would require a mother to identify the father of her child before she receives welfare. It is the pivotal first step in changing human behavior. You cannot foster the development of the family unless you connect the mother and child with the father. The archaic welfare system has actually done the opposite—driving men and women apart. It divides the family.

The 1995 welfare reform bill is a big step forward. But I am hoping we will soon go even further. Freedom means being responsible for yourself. You reap the rewards of your good actions but you also suffer the consequences of your bad actions. Slavery took away the freedom of African Americans and gave responsibility to someone else. Welfare has done the same thing. We African Americans will never be free until we learn to be responsible for ourselves.

TWENTY-THREE

Welfare as a Loan Program

O N THE FLOOR of the U.S. House of Representatives in 1995, I made a speech that rocked some of the members of Congress. I stated that we should look at "real welfare reform." That phrase alone did not grab anyone's attention. After all, everyone from President Clinton on down has been talking about it since the 1992 campaign.

Yet my proposal was different. Instead of patching up the existing system or turning it back to the states, I proposed that we replace welfare with a loan program. Yes, a loan program. When I said that on the floor of the House, people paused to see if I was joking. After my speech, my office received phone calls of support from around the country.

The idea came to me after an encounter I had back in the spring of 1995 in my local barbershop.

"What's going on with welfare reform?" my barber asked me as he snipped at my hair. "My old lady is wondering if you guys are going to leave her homeless and starving to death."

A young man in his twenties was sitting waiting to get his hair cut. "Oh, they ain't doin' [expletive]," he said, before I could answer. "They ain't got the heart to hurt people. It's a big bluff. It's just a game."

"No, man," countered my barber. "I heard the Republicans are mean people and the Republicans want real change."

"Oh, yeah," said the youngster, laughing. "Instead of Marty [his girlfriend, I suppose] getting her check from Washington, she's going to get it from the state of Connecticut. She thought she was getting it from the state of Connecticut anyhow and they still going to pay her rent. It's no big deal."

I did not want to get drawn into the conversation. But the last remark was too much. "No, it will be quite different," I said.

The barber stopped cutting my hair and looked me dead in the eye. "Congressman, I respect you and all that," he said. "It's your debit card idea that'll kick our ass. Now that could really hurt."

"Oh, man," interrupted the young man. "They ain't going to go through with that because too many people would get hurt. People have to have their drugs, you know, they got to have it."

"That's why I believe it will happen," I said. "I strongly believe we will pass the debit card and it will make a big difference in preventing people from using welfare money to buy drugs."

"[Expletive], man. Ain't no way," said the youngster, slouching down in his chair.

I learned a lot from that encounter. It obviously reaffirmed my belief in the benefits of the electronic transfer system. But there was more than that. After my encounter in the barbershop, I felt we had to change the whole nature of the system. That's when I came up with the idea of making welfare a loan program.

The purpose of the loan program would be to change the mind-set of welfare recipients. We need to remind them that we as taxpayers will help those in need of assistance during a downturn in their lives, but we should also expect to get our investment back. There is no free lunch. I want welfare recipients to become part of the real world. All Americans abide by the same principles. If you put nothing in, you should get nothing out. Those who reap now should be expected to help sow in the future.

Totally eliminating welfare as we know it would create a society that does not lose its compassion but expects greater responsibility. We need to correct the misconception that we, the federal government, should be the mother and father of every disadvantaged child. We may be Uncle Sam, but we're not every child's parents.

We should get the extended family involved—the grandmother and grandfather. I realize that after generation after generation of dependency, both grandmother and grandfather may be on welfare themselves. But there are examples where grandparents help children and grandchildren. Those who can should be required to assist.

For most Americans, if you don't work, you don't get paid. The biblical phrase "You reap what you sow" is true for most people but not for welfare recipients. In most of American life, if you need a little help because of a downturn, you can get a loan. Even cities often have to resort to selling bonds. The United States government has been in the borrowing business for thirty years.

But all these borrowers are eventually obligated to pay the money back. Why not demand the same of welfare recipients? When times become better, we would hope our cities, our country, and our welfare recipients would pay back their loans.

How would such a system work? We cannot expect dollar-for-dollar returns. At first we may settle for something like 5 or 10 percent. In Connecticut, welfare recipients receive an estimated $24,000 a year, so that would mean $2,400 would be repayable. Welfare benefits will probably be capped at five years under current welfare reform, so that would be a total of $12,000. The percentage could be raised if it became workable in the future.

The recipients would have three options: (1) pay off the dollars straight out over a reasonable length of time, (2) work the benefits off at an hourly rate while working for an approved non-profit or state-sponsored organization, or (3) any combination of the above. Welfare recipients could work as watchdogs in crime prevention, carrying walkie-talkies but not guns. There is no end to the things able-bodied people can do to help society. Let's be bold and creative.

The biggest benefit would be to the welfare recipients themselves. They would finally be able to say that they are carrying their own weight. The general population would know that they are part of society, making a contribution. It would be a revolutionary change in the idea of social services.

Of course, people would have to qualify for the loan. If one parent has some resources, that could be a factor in denying the loan or increasing the payback from 10 to 30 percent. But that shouldn't stop us. We want to cut the shackles of welfare dependency as rapidly as possible. We want to encourage as many people as possible to strive to become entrepreneurs. We want welfare recipients to be able to do what everyday Americans can do: accumulate assets, own a truck, a typewriter, fax, or Xerox machine. Those items could be used to start a secretarial or lawn-care business. Right now our current system allows none of this because the value of a truck or its equivalent disqualifies a person for welfare.

Many people laugh off such a thought for a welfare recipient. However, there are different kinds of welfare recipients. Some people represent a third or fourth generation. Others have fallen on welfare only recently due to the untimely death of a husband or some other misfortune. The original legislation—Aid to Families with Dependent Children (AFDC)—was intended to provide for a mother and her children due to the death of the father. Today we have stretched that a bit. We take care of the mother and children of the "living-dead" fathers.

Congresswoman Lynn Woolsey of California was on welfare for a short period. Many other people do the same thing. If we deny them an opportunity to better themselves by starting their own business or accumulating assets, we would be denying them an opportunity we afford other Americans. It would not be right.

Interest rates on such loans would be structured like any other bank transaction. There should be little or no restriction on assets. As long as we reserve the right to have 100 percent payback, what difference would accumulating assets make?

I would like to see a mechanism that would allow a welfare recipient to borrow money on terms very similar to a banker's terms—although a bit more expensive, since we do not want to attract people into the program who would go on welfare just to qualify. Typically, by the time a person qualifies for welfare, they have done irrevocable damage to their credit. If a person is not deemed creditworthy, he or she is already relegated to a lifestyle far different from that of most Americans. Granted, it is important for people to live up to their financial obligations, but assistance with correcting one's credit will get a welfare recipient on the road to self-sufficiency more rapidly.

Loans for the poor is a contradiction in terms. We all know that banks seem to give money when you don't need it and deny you money when you need it most. That's where planning comes in. We should realize that all welfare recipients may not be capable of being entrepreneurs, but we can't force them all into McDonald's-like jobs either. Opportunity, hope, showing a path— not putting up unreasonable barriers—are the ways to change behavior.

Now you may say, "Where does the money come from?" There are several possibilities. We could use the capital received from the payback of social service loans as venture capital for business start-ups. A bill I introduced in the 103d Congress—the Welfare Entrepreneur Opportunity Act—makes just this proposal. It is similar to my Urban Entrepreneurs Opportunity Act. The thrust would be to allow the private sector to drive the program.

For many years, welfare has become like the father and grand- father to young mothers and their children. But one good thing fathers and grandfathers usually do is give people confidence that they can do something. Giving welfare recipients access to loan money for a business venture would be a way of saying, "We believe in you." For people who are constantly having doors shut in their faces, this would be long overdue.

TWENTY-FOUR

Debit Cards for Welfare Recipients

ONE DAY ON my way to church recently, I met a woman in her mid-fifties whom I have known for almost twenty years. I realized I hadn't seen her for a long time. She was holding a tiny child in her arms.

"Where've you been lately?" I asked. "I didn't realize you'd become a grandma."

"This is Harry's little boy." She smiled. Then, lowering her voice, she continued, "You know, this crack is a real bad thing. I've never seen a drug like this before. It's killing people."

She seemed to be holding the child too close. "What's wrong with the baby?" I asked.

She opened her arms to reveal an ill-clad child. His T-shirt and socks were far too small and he had no shoes on.

"I can't take care of this baby," she said. "But if I don't try, no one will. I would hate to have this baby go to the state, but I may have to do that."

"Why aren't Harry and his girlfriend taking care of him?" I asked. "Doesn't she get assistance?"

"Yes, but Harry forces her to cash the checks and they use the money to buy crack. They don't take care of the baby. I'm trying to do it all myself but it's hard."

"You should report them to the authorities," I said to her.

She looked at me suspiciously. "I don't dare say anything to them," she said. "They're crazy." She started to leave.

"My Harry is not the only one doing this," she said, looking back. "Everyone is doing it. Everyone." She hugged the baby closer and walked away.

For many years, we have refused to confront the deplorable situation that much of the money given to welfare recipients is being spent on drugs. The problem is nationwide. A Columbia University study recently found that 25 percent of all welfare recipients are drug users.

Shortly after my encounter outside church, the television networks carried the story of twenty people living in a four-room apartment in Chicago. The five adults were all drug abusers. They were also receiving over five thousand dollars a month in welfare benefits. None of the fifteen children were suitably clothed.

I mentioned the problem in the Black Caucus one day to Rep. Harold Ford, then chair of a House Ways and Means subcommittee that was considering welfare reform.

"Shouldn't we try to do something about this?" I asked Ford.

"I believe people are looking at it," he replied. Yet nothing was ever done. It saddens me that people can respond in such a ho-hum fashion.

After studying the problem, I decided the best way to deal with this—and many other problems about welfare—would be to transform welfare benefits into an electronic "debit card." This would work like any other credit card. Welfare recipients would be extended a line of credit at the beginning of the month. They could draw down on their line of credit—but not overdraw.

The important thing is that the card would only be good for certain transactions. Recipients could pay rent and utility bills via electronic transfer. They could buy food at grocery stores and purchase medicine and other necessities. But they would not be able to take out lump sums of cash that could be spent on drugs.

192 ◆ GARY FRANKS

In 1993, I introduced a bill in Congress that would replace cash welfare payments with a debit card. I testified before the Ways and Means Committee and quizzed Secretary of Health and Human Services Donna Shalala when she appeared before the Black Caucus. No one had any serious objections. Shalala even said that she hoped a version of the debit card would be incorporated in the Clinton administration's welfare reform proposal. Still, nothing happened.

In 1994, I emphasized the issue in my reelection campaign for Congress. One of my TV campaign ads showed a young woman at a cash register buying food. Instead of paying cash or food stamps, she pulled out a welfare debit card and gave it to the cashier. I promised that if reelected I would fight to implement this kind of system in the 104th Congress.

Not content to wait for Congress, I approached the Connecticut State Legislature. They agreed to pilot a project in Waterbury.

When the new Republican Congress tackled welfare reform, Congressmen Clay Shaw (R-Fla.) and Bill Emerson (R-Mo.), chairmen of the human resources and agricultural operations subcommittees, respectively, both embraced the idea. A debit-card system was quickly incorporated into the House bill. The Senate bill set up an electronic system for food stamps but not for Aid to Families with Dependent Children (AFDC). The idea was eventually accepted by the Welfare Reform Conference Committee, of which I was a member.

Drug dealers do not take plastic today, but I'm sure they will adapt if an electronic benefits system goes into place. Bartering could also counter our efforts. Any debit-card system will require monitoring. Repeated, large-scale purchases at any suspect location would have to be investigated. The system will leave a paper trail. Coupled with stiff penalties, such a system should prove an effective way to stem the flow of welfare dollars to drug dealers.

Americans account for nearly every penny of government money spent with defense contractors such as Pratt & Whitney, Sikorsky, and Electric Boat. We should do the same with welfare dollars. A debit-card system would not only protect taxpayers' investment but also improve the lives of welfare recipients. It would ensure that the government would provide benefits that would actually go toward the children's basic needs.

TWENTY-FIVE

Housing

IN LOOKING AT changing our welfare system, I am puzzled as to how we do so without seriously addressing a significant portion of the needs of the indigent. It has always been said that food and shelter are the two vital components of everyone's existence. In the Welfare Reform Act of 1995, we have not truly addressed shelter.

The housing of the poor is an integral part of the welfare benefits package. Aid to Families with Dependent Children (AFDC), food stamps, and health care (Medicaid) are the traditional benefits most frequently associated with welfare recipients. However, housing is also a part of the package. It has been estimated that the allotment for a person on welfare in Connecticut would total twenty-four thousand dollars a year. To equal that sum, a working family would have to earn over thirty thousand dollars. Something is wrong with this picture.

If you are a young girl living in a crowded apartment, you can get relief simply by having a baby. The government will give you an apartment. They will automatically increase your cash benefit if you have another one. The taxpayers will cough up the money. Our system rewards negative behavior.

We should not allow minors to have their own apartments simply by having a baby. Nor should we give that young lady more money for having more babies. Try telling your boss you want a raise because you have had another baby in the family. Good luck.

I would strongly encourage radical changes in how we house the poor. The problem with public housing is that it can only serve so many people. There are huge waiting lists at almost every government project throughout the country. As a result, some people get the whole allotment while others get nothing.

Let us review how this actually works:

> Jane Smith receives $900 in cash benefits per month.
> She does not receive a rental allowance.
> Her monthly rent is $400.
> Jane's available cash after rental expense is $500.

> Sally Jones receives $900 in cash benefits per month.
> She receives a rental allowance of $350.
> Her monthly rent is $400.
> Sally's available cash after rental expense is $850.

Why is Sally so fortunate? Maybe she is just lucky or maybe she knows the right people at the local housing authority. Either way, there is an obvious need for greater fairness in housing subsidies. Many people who live in public housing never leave. Some of them are not poor. You are means-tested when you are admitted but you are not always means-tested after that. Thus, public housing becomes a form of rent control. As we look at putting time limits on welfare benefits, we should also look at putting limits on stays in public housing.

I would like to see radical changes that would eventually lead to the total elimination of the Department of Housing and Urban Development (HUD).

1. I would seek to privatize (or demolish where needed) public housing.
2. I would increase the deduction for the low-income housing tax credit.
3. I would restore the passive-loss rules on real estate to what they were before the 1986 Tax Reform Act. These encouraged

apartment construction by allowing real estate investors unlimited use of depreciation and other losses to reduce their tax obligation on other income.

We have to blow up the plantation-style living of twentieth-century public housing and instead make it attractive for investors to get involved in building housing in depressed areas.

One thing that would make housing easier to maintain for private landlords would be the electronic benefits transfer system. Today, all too much welfare money goes to illegal drugs and too little goes to pay the rent. Many landlords will not rent to welfare tenants because they are not sure of receiving the rent checks. Others will rent to welfare tenants but are constantly struggling to collect. An electronic benefits system would allow the welfare office to pay the money directly into the landlord's bank account. Utility bills could be paid in the same way. This will improve upkeep of properties and make it easier for welfare recipients to find apartments. (A system of annual inspection would have to be instituted to certify that the landlord is keeping up the property.)

Prior to the 1986 Tax Reform Act, doctors, lawyers, corporate executives, and others were encouraged to invest in low-income housing around the country. There was no cap on the amount of money one could deduct for debt service and other rental property expenses. When that changed, so did the housing market. Low-income housing was the most adversely affected. To bring investors back into the market, we must return to the pre-1986 tax laws.

As you already know, my family's climb from being hourly wage workers into the middle class began when my father bought a three-decker house. Howard Hussock, a housing expert with the Kennedy School of Government, has written that the three-decker is the solution to the nation's housing problem. I believe from experience that he is right.

What's so special about the three-decker? First, it allowed someone like my father, a nearly illiterate factory worker, to own his own home. That was no small thing. Sure, we were making monthly mortgage payments to the bank, just as tenants make monthly payments to the landlord. But we were also investing.

"What you owe today you will be worth tomorrow" is an old saying in real estate. It doesn't work if you borrow money to buy a car or a new stereo or to pay the groceries—as the federal government has been doing, in effect, for the last thirty years. But if you invest in something that has permanent value—"real estate"—your debt payments will eventually be repaid in the value of your property. In addition, your interest payments are tax-deductible, and you can realize a depreciation tax benefit.

At one time in the 1980s, I owned properties worth two to three million dollars—on paper, at least. That was a long way from the little three-decker that my father bought in 1952. But I accumulated them in basically the same way. I bought properties with bank loans, improved them, and then paid down the mortgage largely through rents collected from the tenants.

You're doing something else as well. You're providing housing to people who can't afford to buy their own homes. In our three-decker, we had tenants who were good friends on the top floor and relatives on the bottom. Lots of people do it that way. Whole regions of our cities were once filled with multifamily homes where struggling families like ours were slowly making their way up the ladder by providing housing services for one another.

The last thing a landlord wants in his building is a drug dealer. Drug dealers will terrorize other tenants, bring all kinds of dangerous people into the building, and generally give the place a bad reputation. The good tenants are soon going to be moving out.

The problem is that many states have now passed tough eviction laws that make it very difficult to get people out. Drug dealers are often the most skilled people at using these laws—and if they're not, they may have Legal Services attorneys to help them. The result is that a private landlord often can't keep his building clean and safe even if he wants to.

However bad the problem is for private landlords, it is much worse in public housing. It used to be that you couldn't live in many public housing projects if you had a relative in prison. Single mothers were generally banned before the 1960s. Today it may take years to evict a street gang that is openly dealing drugs. Jack Kemp made a noble effort to change these policies when he was secretary of housing and urban development, but the momentum is all the other way. Government makes a distant, bureaucratic landlord and Legal Services Corporation attorneys continue to tie the system in knots.

One aspect of the current public housing approach should be continued. Many public housing complexes have been working with tenants to help them manage the upkeep of their unit. That would not be needed in the privatized units.

I would also applaud assistance in the financial planning area for the indigent. Ideally, nonprofit family development organizations or an organized volunteer effort could allow us to fill this void. Handling money can be difficult even for the best of us. Most welfare recipients do not have role models. The goal should be to help make a dependent person independent via the use of carrots and sticks.

Let us not forget that many people in public housing feel trapped, much as the slaves felt when they were on the plantation. It is unfortunate that it is so easy to draw comparisons between today's welfare and slavery. We ended slavery, we should at least work our way toward the same goal for welfare. Slaves had little or no hope. Slaves were totally dependent on their masters. Slaves were not in full control of their destiny. Our welfare system has created generation after generation of dependent people. There are a number of obvious differences. For one, slaves were black while welfare recipients are mostly white (though a disproportionate number are African Americans). But the result is the same.

As a conservative Republican, I have always advocated less government involvement. In its place, the tax structure should provide appropriate incentives for those capable of providing a worthy service or product. Let's keep in mind that with any government-run program, there are administrative costs. Let us do away with the current structure and use the money in a way that eliminates the middle man while providing greater or better services.

Instead of warehousing people on welfare, we could be assimilating them into the general population. This will once again make the ultimate transition to independence more likely.

PART FIVE

MY CREDO

TWENTY-SIX

Faith in God

As a child, I was always told to respect the basic principles of the Bible. The Ten Commandments were taught to me early in life. They instilled in me the deep conviction that I should obey the laws of God. There was an ever-present fear that God would punish those who did not abide by His teachings.

My closeness to God is why I consider myself so blessed, or rather, "lucky." The "fluke" that my critics often make my election out to be is the result of nothing more than God guiding and bestowing His goodwill upon me. I fear not only the retribution that I could receive on earth for doing wrong but, more importantly, the prospects of having my soul cast into hell for an eternity.

It's unfortunate that so many people fail to believe that you will be blessed if you treat your neighbor the way you would want to be treated yourself. So many people fail to believe that they will be punished or receive ill fortune if they hurt others. God has a way of making this become a reality.

I strongly believe that if an atheist were to follow me around for a year, he would become a believer in God. He would be persuaded to adhere to the law of God—the Ten Commandments—and would aspire to live in the Kingdom of God in Heaven.

Imagine what kind of world this would be if we all competed to outperform our neighbor in adhering to the Ten Commandments. Today many people rationalize their evil or corrupt practices. They tell themselves "I won't get caught," "Everybody does it," or "I will only do this one time." In every way, they are wrong. Their evil and corrupt ways compound one another to the point where greed and selfishness dominate their lifestyle. They use the word *love* only in the context of material things.

It should be remembered that if you love your mother and father, you obey them and respect them. You give of your time to be with them, to share things with them. If you truly want to show your love for God, you obey Him, you spend time with Him, you visit His house (church) as often as you can. You share things with Him by expressing your gratitude for His many blessings.

Many people feel that such "good guys" are bound to finish last. Well, I am able to attest that one can rise from very humble beginnings to high levels by doing right. Abiding by the Ten Commandments, loving others as much as you love yourself, praying for your enemies instead of hating them—it all works.

I never worry about punishing or attacking my enemies. I work hard to do right myself. I go out of my way to help people, much as my beloved parents Richard and Jenary Franks did. I've volunteered my time in soup kitchens and civic groups and have visited the sick in hospitals. We all have a responsibility to give of ourselves while expecting nothing in return other than the satisfaction of knowing you have helped someone or that you have made someone's day a little brighter. For many, this practice does not have to start with strangers. It could start with your own family or circle of friends.

It is also incumbent upon us to believe in ourselves and to have the courage to fight for what we believe in no matter how unpopular it may be. God never gives you more than you can handle, and often with growth comes a little pain. We should realize that failures and rejections are ways in which God directs, tests, and strengthens us. If I had been elected state comptroller or state party chairman as I first hoped, I probably would not be sitting in Congress today.

Yes, I have had temporary failures, but I know that you never lose until you quit. I always realized that I would have another day to try again. God willing, I would succeed, maybe not in the way I originally hoped but in a way that was ultimately better. Patience is truly a virtue.

I believe that God has a plan for all of us. It is how we live our lives that determines which path we will be on. Some people seem to go in circles, some people seem to go backward, and some people seem placed on the route of success. Most importantly, you determine your own fate as a reflection of God's attitude toward the way you are leading your life.

It should also be noted that we must work hard. We must pay our dues, plant our seeds, sacrifice in order to reap rewards. If you put nothing in the ground, you cannot expect to get something out.

Those who refuse to recognize this will probably fail. They will lose control of their lives and become dependent on others for their existence.

For far too long, the African American community has been focused on how "we have been done wrong." We should focus instead on our strengths. We should be building our families, our neighborhoods, our communities. By doing so, we will no longer have to look toward Uncle Sam as we have done in the past.

Even during slavery, African Americans maintained the strength of the church and the belief in a superior being, God Almighty, maker of Heaven and Earth. Yet attendance in black churches has been in a steady decline since the 1960s.

Families are like teams. Successful teams stick together. Successful teams believe in themselves. Families and teams help each other out, protect each other, know the strengths and weaknesses of each member.

Families are made up of individuals. Individuals should believe in themselves and recognize their strengths and weaknesses in order to derive the most out of their abilities. Individuals should seek help, guidance, and inner strength from God, just as members of families and teams receive support from one another.

Families make up communities. Individuals, families, and communities prosper when we adhere to the aforementioned principles. Not believing in yourself, hating or hurting yourself or your family, and having no love for your community result in a disastrous condition. Hopelessness, despair, frustration, and anger will manifest themselves prominently.

Imagine if 250 black-owned companies along with the top 250 wealthiest black men and women (sports figures, entertainers, and businesspeople) would contribute $250,000 to $1 million a year to a nonprofit "self-help" organization to help blacks start their own businesses. Five hundred million dollars would be invested every year in the black community.

Fidelity is the key to a successful marriage. In this respect, my lovely wife, Donna, truly has nothing to worry about. Yes, I love her dearly and feel as though she has played a major role in shaping my life since the day we met. When I married her in 1990, I was convinced that she was the woman with whom I wanted to spend the rest of my life. I was convinced that she was the woman I wanted to be the mother of my children. Today I have been blessed with Jessica Lynn, born in June 1991, Gary Jr., born in May 1994, and my stepdaughter, Azia, born in May 1984. Though no one knows what the future may hold and politicians frequently get divorced, Donna would have to divorce me because I would never divorce her. And, though I am not always charming, I can assure you that adultery would never be the reason for a divorce.

Unfortunately, many of our youth do not fear the police or their parents or God. They have little respect for life itself. They have no appreciation of or faith in the hereafter.

This represents a fundamental change in our culture from the 1950s to the 1990s. It is part of the erosion of the family, especially among African Americans.

Tied closely to the feeling of faith is the concept of hope. You have to not only hope and dream but also believe that, no matter what, you will be able to achieve your dreams. It is a matter of believing in something that you cannot see or prove. Many times, like Doubting Thomas, I pray to God to increase my faith. With God all things are possible.

Who would have thought that Moses would be able to lead the Hebrews away from the control of the Egyptian Pharaoh?

Who would have thought that Moses, born a slave, would be

raised by Pharaoh? Likewise, many of my forefathers never dreamed that slavery could end without them lifting a finger in combat.

Yes, there is a God. Baptist ministers often repeat the old adage that God may not always be there when you want Him but He is always right on time.

I strongly support school prayer. As a youngster in public grade school, I always participated in some form of meditation. In parochial school, we started every class and athletic event with a prayer.

I try hard to recognize the Sabbath as a day of rest, God's day. After my election to Congress, I informed my towns and cities that I would not participate in Sunday events unless they were family-related events. I personally regret that we allow so much commerce to take place on Sunday. As a child, I can remember stores being closed on Sunday. If God could rest on the Sabbath after making Heaven and Earth as well as all living creatures, we should at least try to do the same.

I would also encourage people to read the Bible regularly. It is enlightening and comforting. Along with going to church, it strengthens my resolve. I read the Bible daily. Bringing people back to God is a difficult thing to do. It takes those who have been blessed to communicate the wonders of God to those whose faith may be weak or nonexistent.

Getting people to respect and love others will go a long way toward repairing a society that is so frequently driven by hatred and despair. When I think of the concept of law and order in a civilized society, I cannot imagine living life without rules. It would be barbaric. But just imagine what the world would be like if everyone feared God and lived by the Ten Commandments. What a world that would be. Just to show what it would be like, I would like to list the Ten Commandments:

> Thou shalt love the Lord thy God with all thy heart and with all thy soul and all thy might. Thou shalt have no other gods before me.

Thou shalt not make unto thee any graven image, nor
    bow down unto them, nor worship them.
Thou shalt not take the name of the Lord thy God in vain.
Remember the Sabbath Day and keep it holy.
Honor thy father and thy mother.
Thou shalt not kill.
Thou shalt not commit adultery.
Thou shalt not steal.
Thou shalt not bear false witness against thy neighbor.
Thou shalt not covet thy neighbor's house, nor his wife,
    nor his manservant, nor his maidservant, nor his ox, nor
    his ass, nor anything that is thy neighbor's.

If everyone lived by these principles, the misery and despair
we live with would meet their match.

EPILOGUE

RACE BAITERS and hate mongers come in all stripes and colors. Given enough room, they could destroy this country from within. They are the obvious enemy in our search for the promised land. But good people who are not willing to fight, or even to support other people who are waging the good battle, are also impeding our progress.

We may all realize how far we have come as a nation, as a people. But we do not seem to realize just how close we are to reaching the promised land if we recommit ourselves to the values that have made America the envy of the world. Such a commitment would ensure that we would only be limited by the extent of our dreams. This is a great nation made up of great people.

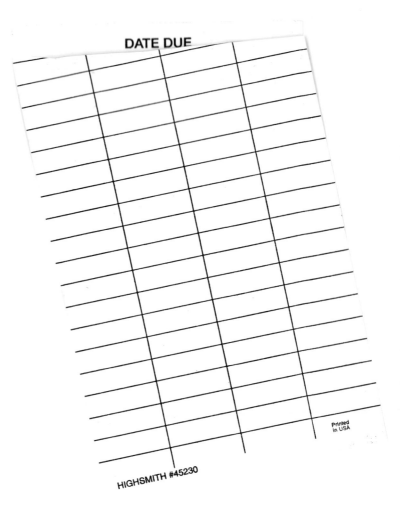

DATE DUE

Printed
in USA

HIGHSMITH #45230